Memory
and Identity

Donated by

Colusa Lions Club

2007

Memory
and Identity

Conversations
at the Dawn of a Millennium

Pope John Paul II

THORNDIKE
CHIVERS

This Large Print edition is published by Thorndike Press®, Waterville, Maine USA and by BBC Audiobooks Ltd, Bath, England.

Published in 2005 in the U.S. by arrangement with Rizzoli International Publications, Inc.

Published in 2006 in the U.K. by arrangement with Orion Publishing Group Ltd.

U.S. Hardcover   0-7862-8029-8 (Inspirational)
U.K. Hardcover   1-4056-3465-0 (Chivers Large Print)
U.K. Softcover   1-4056-3466-9 (Camden Large Print)

The original title of the work is:
Pamięć i tożsamość. Rozmowy na przełomie tysiącleci
Copyright © 2005 Libreria Editrice Vaticana, Città del Vaticano
Copyright © 2005 RCS Libri S.p.A., Milano
Originally published in Italian in 2005 by RCS Libri S.p.A.
–Rizzoli, Milan

The text of this Large Print edition is unabridged.
Other aspects of the book may vary from the original edition.

Set in 16 pt. Plantin by Al Chase.

Printed in the United States on permanent paper.

ISBN 0-7862-8029-8 (lg. print : hc : alk. paper)

Memory and Identity

Contents

THE LIMIT IMPOSED UPON EVIL 17

1. *Mysterium Iniquitatis:* The
   Coexistence of Good and Evil   19
2. Ideologies of Evil   22
3. The Limit Imposed Upon Evil
   in European History   34
4. Redemption as the Divine Limit
   Imposed Upon Evil   38
5. The Mystery of Redemption   45
6. Redemption: Victory Given as
   a Task to Man   49

FREEDOM AND RESPONSIBILITY 55

7. Toward a Just Use of Freedom   57
8. Freedom Is for Love   65
9. The Lessons of Recent History   71
10. The Mystery of Mercy   79

THINKING "MY COUNTRY"
(NATIVE LAND — NATION —
STATE)   87

11. On the Concept of *Patria*
    (Native Land)   89
12. Patriotism   97
13. The Concept of Nation   101
14. History   107
15. Nation and Culture   114

THINKING "EUROPE"
(POLAND — EUROPE —
CHURCH)   129

16. Europe as "Native Land"   131
17. The Evangelization of Central
    and Eastern Europe   145
18. The Positive Fruits of the
    Enlightenment   154
19. The Mission of the Church   165
20. The Relationship Between
    Church and State   170
21. Europe in the Context of
    Other Continents   174

DEMOCRACY: POSSIBILITIES
AND RISKS   179

22. Modern Democracy   181
23. Back to Europe?   191
24. The Maternal Memory of
    the Church   204

25. The Vertical Dimension of
     European History   213

    EPILOGUE   219

26. "Someone Must Have Guided
     That Bullet"   221

Notes   235

Editorial Note

The twentieth century witnessed historical events that marked a decisive change in the political and social situation of entire nations, and significantly influenced the destinies of individual citizens. It is now sixty years since the end of the war that engulfed the world in a tragic drama of destruction and death from 1939 until 1945. Subsequent years saw the spread of Communist dictatorship into several Central and Eastern European nations and the growth of Marxist ideology in other parts of Europe, Africa, Latin America, and Asia. Sadly, the opening years of the twenty-first century have been clouded by the spread of terrorism on a global scale: the destruction of the World Trade Center in New York provides the most striking example. How can we fail to see in these events the active presence of the *mysterium iniquitatis?*

Alongside evil, however, there has been much that is good. The dictatorships established behind the "iron curtain" did not extinguish the yearning for liberty on the part of the oppressed peoples. In Poland, despite government opposition, the trade union movement known as *Solidarność* was formed. It was a rallying call, which found echoes elsewhere. Then came 1989, which has passed into history as the year when the Berlin Wall fell, leading to the rapid collapse of the decades-old Communist regimes in Central and Eastern Europe. The twentieth century also witnessed the attainment of independence by many nations previously under colonial rule. New states came to birth, and whatever pressures and restrictions they may still experience, they now enjoy the freedom to choose their own destiny. Since the Second World War, various international organizations have been established with the task of promoting the peace and security of peoples. These agencies are committed to working for a more equitable distribution of the world's resources, for the protection of the rights of individuals, and for the recognition of the legitimate aspirations of different social groups. Finally, mention should be made of the birth and subsequent growth of the European Union.

The life of the Church has also witnessed eventful changes that have inspired significant growth and renewal for the present and also, one hopes, for the future of the People of God. Among these events, pride of place must surely go to the Second Vatican Council (1962–1965) and to the various initiatives that followed: the liturgical reform, the establishment of new pastoral agencies, the great missionary outreach, the commitment to ecumenism and inter-religious dialogue, to mention only the more important among them. And let us not underestimate the great spiritual and ecclesial benefits that followed from the celebration of the Great Jubilee of the Year 2000.

A significant witness of all these developments is Pope John Paul II. He experienced firsthand the dramatic and heroic events of his own country, Poland, to which he remains deeply attached. In recent decades he has also played a leading role — first as a priest, then as a Bishop, and now as Pope — in many important developments in the history of Europe and of the whole world. This book offers an insight into his experiences and the fruit of his reflections, born amid so much evil, yet grounded in his firm belief that the power of good ultimately prevails. In his assessment of various aspects of current affairs expressed in a series of "conversations at the dawn of a millennium," the

Holy Father has reflected on present realities in the light of the past, seeking the roots of what is happening now, so as to offer his contemporaries, both individuals and nations, the opportunity to arrive through "memory" at a keener awareness of their true "identity."

In writing this book, John Paul II returned to the main themes of some conversations that took place in 1993 in Castel Gandolfo. Two Polish philosophers, Józef Tischner and Krzysztof Michalski, founders of the Vienna-based Institute for Human Sciences (*Institut für die Wissenschaften vom Menschen*), invited him to undertake a critical analysis, from a historical and philosophical point of view, of the two dictatorships that marked twentieth-century Polish history: nazism and communism. Those conversations were recorded and subsequently transcribed. In returning to them now, the Holy Father has sought to enlarge the perspective of the discussion. Beginning from these conversations, he has gone further, setting the reflections in a broader context. The result is the present book, which addresses certain themes crucial for the destiny of mankind, a few years into the third millennium.

This book uses the literary form of a conversation, so that the reader may more easily appreciate that it is not an academic treatise but an informal dialogue. While problems are considered rigorously in search of appropriate solutions, no attempt is made to provide an exhaustive analysis. The questions in their present form are editorial. They are intended to engage the reader's attention, helping him to follow the Holy Father's train of thought. It is hoped that everyone who reads this book will find here answers to at least some of the questions that he carries in his heart.

THE LIMIT
IMPOSED UPON EVIL

1. *Mysterium Iniquitatis:* The Coexistence of Good and Evil

After the fall of the two powerful totalitarian systems which overshadowed the whole of the twentieth century and were responsible for innumerable crimes — nazism in Germany and "real socialism" in the Soviet Union — it seems that the time has come for a reflection on their causes, their effects, and especially on the significance of the ideologies they introduced into the history of mankind. Holy Father, what is the meaning of this great "eruption" of evil?

The twentieth century was, so to speak, the "theater" in which particular historical and ideological processes were played out, leading toward that great "eruption" of evil, but it also provided the setting for their defeat. Is it fair, then, to consider Europe solely from the point of view of the evil which marked its recent history? Is this not a rather one-sided approach? The modern history of Europe, shaped — especially in the West — by the influence of the Enlightenment, has yielded many positive fruits. This is actually characteristic of evil, as understood by Saint Thomas, following in the tradition of Saint Augustine. Evil is always the absence of some good which ought to be present in a given being; it is a privation. It is never a total absence of good. The way in which evil grows from the pure soil of good is a mystery. Another mystery is the element of good which is never destroyed by evil and which keeps on growing despite it, sometimes even from the same soil. The Gospel parable of the good grain and the weeds comes to mind immediately (cf. Mt 13:24–30). When the servants ask the householder: "Do you want us to go and gather them [the weeds]?", his reply is highly significant: "No, for in gathering the weeds you would uproot the wheat along with them. Let both of them grow together until the harvest; and at harvest time I will tell the reapers, 'Collect the weeds first and bind them in bundles to be burned, but gather the wheat into my barn' " (Mt 13:29–30). In this case, the reference to the harvest points to the final phase of history, the *eschaton*.

This parable can serve as a key to the entire history of mankind. In different eras and in different ways, "wheat" grows alongside "weeds" and "weeds" alongside "wheat." The history of mankind is the "theater" of the coexistence of good and evil. So even if evil exists alongside good, good perseveres beside evil and grows, so to speak, from the same soil, namely human nature. This has not been destroyed, and has not become totally corrupt, despite original sin. Nature has retained its capacity for good, as history confirms.

2. Ideologies of Evil

How, then, did the ideologies of evil originate? What are the roots of nazism and communism? Why did they fail?

These questions have a profound philosophical and theological significance. We need to reconstruct the "philosophy of evil" in its European and extra-European dimensions. This reconstruction will take us beyond the realm of ideology and into the world of faith. We need to consider the mystery of God, the mystery of creation and, in particular, the mystery of man. In the first few years of my ministry as Successor of Peter, I tried to express these three mysteries through the encyclicals *Redemptor Hominis*, *Dives in Misericordia*, and *Dominum et Vivificantem*. This triptych explores the Trinitarian mystery of God. Everything I said in the encyclical *Redemptor Hominis* I brought with me from Poland. Likewise, the reflections offered in *Dives in Misericordia* were the fruit of my pastoral experience in Poland, especially in Kraków. That is where Saint Faustina Kowalska is buried, she who was chosen by Christ to be a particularly enlightened interpreter of the truth of Divine Mercy. For Sister Faustina, this truth led to an extraordinarily rich mystical life. She was a simple, uneducated person, and yet those who read the *Diary* of her revelations are astounded by the depth of her mystical experience.

I mention Sister Faustina because her revelations, focused on the mystery of Divine Mercy, occurred during the period preceding the Second World War. This was precisely the time when those ideologies of evil, nazism and communism, were taking shape. Sister Faustina became the herald of the one message capable of off-setting the evil of those ideologies, the fact that God is Mercy — the truth of the merciful Christ. And for this reason, when I was called to the See of Peter, I felt impelled to pass on those experiences of a fellow Pole that deserve a place in the treasury of the universal Church.

The encyclical on the Holy Spirit, *Dominum et Vivificantem*, was conceived a little later: it had its gestation in Rome. It developed during meditation on Saint John's Gospel, on the words spoken by

Jesus during the Last Supper. It was in those final hours of Christ's earthly life that we were given perhaps the most complete revelation on the Holy Spirit. One passage from that farewell discourse is highly significant for the question we are considering. Jesus says that the Holy Spirit "will convince the world concerning sin" (Jn 16:8). As I tried to penetrate these words, I was led back to the opening pages of the Book of Genesis, to the event known as "original sin." Saint Augustine, with extraordinary perceptiveness, described the nature of this sin as follows: *amor sui usque ad contemptum Dei* — self-love to the point of contempt for God.[1] It was *amor sui* which drove our first parents toward that initial rebellion and then gave rise to the spread of sin throughout human history. The Book of Genesis speaks of this: "you will be like God, knowing good and evil" (Gn 3:5), in other words, you yourselves will decide what is good and what is evil.

The only way to overcome this dimension of original sin is through a corresponding *amor Dei usque ad contemptum sui* — love for God to the point of contempt of self. This brings us face to face with the mystery of man's redemption, and here the Holy Spirit is our guide. It is he who allows us to penetrate deeply into the *mysterium Crucis* and at the same time to plumb the depths of the evil perpetrated by man and suffered by man from the very beginning of his history. That is what the expression "convince the world about sin" means, and the purpose of this "convincing" is not to condemn the world. If the Church, through the power of the Holy Spirit, can call evil by its name, it does so only in order to demonstrate that evil can be overcome if we open ourselves to *amor Dei usque ad contemptum sui*. This is the fruit of Divine Mercy. In Jesus Christ, God bends down over man to hold out a hand to him, to raise him up, and to help him continue his journey with renewed strength. Man cannot get back onto his feet unaided: he needs the help of the Holy Spirit. If he refuses this help, he commits what Christ called "the blasphemy against the Spirit," the sin which "will not be forgiven" (Mt 12:31). Why will it not be forgiven? Because it means there is no desire for pardon. Man refuses the love and the mercy of God, since he believes himself to be God. He believes himself to be capable of self-sufficiency.

I have referred briefly to the three encyclicals, which seem to me to offer a fitting commentary on the entire teaching of the

Second Vatican Council, and also on the complexity of the historical period in which we live.

Over the years I have become more and more convinced that the ideologies of evil are profoundly rooted in the history of European philosophical thought. Here I should mention some aspects of European history, and especially its dominant cultural trends. When the encyclical on the Holy Spirit was published, there were some sharply negative reactions from certain quarters in the West. What prompted these reactions? They arose from the same sources as the so-called European Enlightenment over two centuries earlier — particularly the French Enlightenment, though that is not to exclude the English, German, Spanish, and Italian versions. The Enlightenment in Poland followed a path all its own. Russia, on the other hand, apparently escaped the upheaval of the Enlightenment. There, the crisis of Christian tradition arrived from a different direction, erupting at the beginning of the twentieth century with even greater violence in the form of the radically atheist Marxist revolution.

In order to illustrate this phenomenon better, we have to go back to the period before the Enlightenment, especially to the revolution brought about by the philosophical thought of Descartes. The *cogito, ergo sum* (I think, therefore I am) radically changed the way of doing philosophy. In the pre-Cartesian period, philosophy, that is to say the *cogito,* or rather the *cognosco,* was subordinate to *esse,* which was considered prior. To Descartes, however, the *esse* seemed secondary, and he judged the *cogito* to be prior. This not only changed the direction of philosophizing, but it marked the decisive abandonment of what philosophy had been hitherto, particularly the philosophy of Saint Thomas Aquinas, and namely the philosophy of *esse.* Previously, everything was interpreted from the perspective of *esse* and an explanation for everything was sought from the same standpoint. God as fully Self-sufficient Being (*Ens subsistens*) was believed to be the necessary ground of every *ens non subsistens, ens participatum,* that is, of all created beings, including man. The *cogito, ergo sum* marked a departure from that line of thinking. Now the *ens cogitans* enjoyed priority. After Descartes, philosophy became a science of pure thought: all *esse* — both the created world and the Creator — remained within the ambit of the *cogito* as the content of human consciousness.

Philosophy now concerned itself with beings *qua* content of consciousness and not *qua* existing independently of it.

At this point it is worth pausing to examine the traditions of Polish philosophy, especially what happened after the Communist party came to power. In the universities, every form of philosophical thought that did not correspond to the Marxist model was subjected to severe restrictions, and this was done in the simplest and most radical way: by taking action against the people who represented other approaches to philosophy. Foremost among those who were removed from teaching posts were the representatives of realist philosophy, including exponents of realist phenomenology like Roman Ingarden and also Izydora Dąmbska of the Lviv-Warsaw school. It was more difficult to deal with the exponents of Thomism, since they were based at the Catholic University of Lublin and the Theology Faculties of Warsaw and Kraków, as well as the major seminaries, but they too eventually fell victim to the merciless hand of the regime. Certain eminent thinkers who maintained a critical attitude toward dialectical materialism were also regarded with suspicion. Of these I particularly remember Tadeusz Kotarbiński, Maria

Ossowska, and Tadeusz Czeżowski. Clearly it was not possible to remove from the university's teaching program such courses as logic and the methodology of science; yet in different ways the "dissident" professors could be subjected to restrictions, thus limiting by every possible means their influence on students.

What happened in Poland after the Marxists came to power had much the same effect as the philosophical developments that occurred in Western Europe in the wake of the Enlightenment. People spoke, among other things, of the "decline of Thomistic realism" and this was understood to include the abandonment of Christianity as a source for philosophizing. Specifically, the very possibility of attaining to God was placed in question. According to the logic of *cogito, ergo sum,* God was reduced to an element within human consciousness; no longer could he be considered the ultimate explanation of the human *sum.* Nor could he remain as *Ens subsistens,* or "Self-sufficient Being," as the Creator, the one who gives existence, and least of all as the one who gives himself in the mystery of the Incarnation, the Redemption, and grace. The God of Revelation had ceased to exist as "God of the philosophers." All that remained was the idea of God, a topic for free exploration by human thought.

In this way, the foundations of the "philosophy of evil" also collapsed. Evil, in a realist sense, can only exist in relation to good and, in particular, in relation to God, the supreme Good. This is the evil of which the Book of Genesis speaks. It is from this perspective that original sin can be understood, and likewise all personal sin. This evil was redeemed by Christ on the Cross. To be more precise, man was redeemed and came to share in the life of God through Christ's saving work. All this, the entire drama of salvation history, had disappeared as far as the Enlightenment was concerned. Man remained alone: alone as creator of his own history and his own civilization; alone as one who decides what is good and what is bad, as one who would exist and operate *etsi Deus non daretur,* even if there were no God.

If man can decide by himself, without God, what is good and what is bad, he can also determine that a group of people is to be annihilated. Decisions of this kind were taken, for example, by those who came to power in the Third Reich by democratic means, only to misuse their power in order to implement the wicked programs of National Socialist ideology based on racist principles. Similar decisions were also taken by the Communist party in the Soviet Union and in other countries subject to Marxist ideology. This was the context for the extermination of the Jews, and also of other groups, like the Romany peoples, Ukrainian peasants, and Orthodox and Catholic clergy in Russia, in Belarus, and beyond the Urals. Likewise all those who were "inconvenient" for the regime were persecuted; for example, the ex-combatants of September 1939, the soldiers of the National Army in Poland after the Second World War, and those among the intelligentsia who did not share Marxist or Nazi ideology. Normally this meant physical elimination, but sometimes moral elimination: the person would be more or less drastically impeded in the exercise of his rights.

At this point, we cannot remain silent regarding a tragic question that is more pressing today than ever. The fall of the regimes built on ideologies of evil put an end to the forms of extermination just mentioned in the countries concerned. However, there remains the legal extermination of human beings conceived but unborn. And in this case, that extermination is decreed by democratically elected parliaments, which invoke the notion of civil progress for society and for all humanity. Nor are other grave violations of God's law lacking. I am thinking, for example, of the strong pressure from the European Parliament to recognize homosexual unions as an alternative type of family, with the right to adopt children. It is legitimate and even necessary to ask whether this is not the work of another ideology of evil, more subtle and hidden, perhaps, intent upon exploiting human rights themselves against man and against the family.

Why does all this happen? What is the root of these post-Enlightenment ideologies? The answer is simple: it happens because of the rejection of God *qua* Creator, and consequently *qua* source determining what is good and what is evil. It happens because of the rejection of what ultimately constitutes us as human beings, that is, the notion of human nature as a "given reality"; its place has been taken by a "product of thought" freely formed and freely changeable according to circumstances. I believe that a more careful study of this question could lead us beyond the Cartesian watershed. If we wish to speak rationally about good and evil, we have to return to Saint

Thomas Aquinas, that is, to the philosophy of being. With the phenomenological method, for example, we can study experiences of morality, religion, or simply what it is to be human, and draw from them a significant enrichment of our knowledge. Yet we must not forget that all these analyses implicitly presuppose the reality of the Absolute Being and also the reality of being human, that is, being a creature. If we do not set out from such "realist" presuppositions, we end up in a vacuum.

3. The Limit Imposed Upon Evil in European History

Evil sometimes seems omnipotent, it seems to exercise absolute dominion over the world. In your view, Holy Father, does there exist a threshold that evil is unable to cross?

I have had personal experience of ideologies of evil. It remains indelibly fixed in my memory. First there was nazism. What we could see in those years was terrible enough. Yet many aspects of nazism were still hidden at that stage. The full extent of the evil that was raging through Europe was not seen by everyone, not even by those of us situated at the epicenter. We were totally swallowed up in a great eruption of evil and only gradually did we begin to realize its true nature. Those responsible took great pains to conceal their misdeeds from the eyes of the world. Both the Nazis during the war and, later, the Communists in Eastern Europe tried to hide what they were doing from public opinion. For a long time, the West was unwilling to believe in the extermination of the Jews. Only later did this come fully to light. Not even in Poland did we know all that the Nazis had done and were still doing to the Poles, nor what the Soviets had done to the Polish officials in Katyń; and the appalling tragedy of the deportations was still known only in part.

Later, when the war was over, I thought to myself: the Lord God allowed nazism twelve years of existence, and after twelve years the system collapsed. Evidently this was the limit imposed by Divine Providence upon that sort of folly. In truth, it was worse than folly — it was "bestiality," as Konstanty Michalski wrote.[2] Yet the fact is that Divine Providence allowed that bestial fury to be unleashed for only those twelve years. If communism had survived for longer and if it still had the prospect of further development to come, I thought to myself at the time, there had to be meaning in all this.

In 1945, at the end of the war, communism seemed very solid and extremely dangerous — much more so than before. In 1920 we had had the distinct impression that the Communists would conquer Poland and advance farther into Western Europe, poised for world domination. In fact, of course, it never came to that. "The miracle on the Vistula," that is, the triumph of Piłsudski in the battle against the Red Army, muted those Soviet ambitions. After the victory over nazism in 1945, though, the Communists felt reinvigorated and they shamelessly set out to conquer the world, or at least Europe. At first, this led to the re-partition of the Continent into different spheres of influence, according to the agreement reached at Yalta in February 1945. The Communists merely paid lip service to this agreement; in reality, they violated it in various ways, above all through their ideological invasion and political propaganda both in Europe and elsewhere in the world. Even then I knew at once that Communist domination would last much longer than the Nazi occupation had done. For how long? It was hard to predict. There was a sense that this evil was in some way necessary for the world and for mankind. It can happen, in fact, that in certain concrete situations, evil is revealed as somehow useful, inasmuch as it creates opportunities for good. Did not Johann Wolfgang von Goethe describe the devil as *"ein Teil von jener Kraft / die stets das Böse will und stets das Gute schafft"*?[3] Saint Paul, for his part, has this to say: "Do not be overcome by evil, but overcome evil with good"

(Rom 12:21). That, after all, is the way to bring about a greater good in response to evil.

If I have wanted to underline the limit imposed upon evil in European history, I must conclude that the limit is constituted by good — the divine good and the human good that have been revealed in that history, over the course of the last century and of entire millennia. Yet it is hard to forget the evil that has been personally experienced: one can only forgive. And what does it mean to forgive, if not to appeal to a good that is greater than any evil? This good, after all, has its foundation in God alone. Only God is this good. The limit imposed upon evil by divine good has entered human history, especially the history of Europe, through the work of Christ. So it is impossible to separate Christ from human history. This is exactly what I said during my first visit to Poland, in Victory Square, Warsaw. I stated then that it was impossible to separate Christ from my country's history. Is it possible to separate him from any other country's history? Is it possible to separate him from the history of Europe? Only in him, in fact, can all nations and all humanity "cross the threshold of hope"!

4. Redemption as the Divine Limit Imposed Upon Evil

How precisely are we to understand this limit on evil that we have been discussing? What is the essence of this limit?

When I speak of the limit imposed upon evil, I am thinking, above all, of the historical limit Providence imposed upon the evil totalitarian systems established in the twentieth century, namely national socialism and Marxist communism. Yet I find myself wanting at this point to explore some further reflections of a theological nature. I do not simply mean what is sometimes described as a "theology of history." Rather, I mean a deeper theological reflection, analyzing the roots of evil in order to discover how it can be overcome through Christ's saving work.

It is God himself who can place a definitive limit upon evil. He is the essence of justice, because it is he who rewards good and punishes evil in a manner perfectly befitting the objective situation. I am speaking here

38

of moral evil, of sin. In the Garden of Eden, human history already encounters the God who judges and punishes. The Book of Genesis describes in detail the penalty imposed on our first parents after their sin (cf. Gn 3:14–19). And their penalty has been prolonged throughout human history. Original sin is an inherited condition. As such, it signifies the innate sinfulness of man, his radical inclination toward evil instead of good. There is in man a congenital moral weakness which goes hand in hand with the fragility of his being, with his psycho-physical fragility. And this fragility is accompanied by the multiple sufferings indicated in the Bible, from the very first pages, as punishment for sin.

It could be said that human history is marked from the very beginning by the limit God the Creator places upon evil. The Second Vatican Council has much to say on this subject in the pastoral constitution *Gaudium et Spes*. It would be worth quoting the introductory account given in that document concerning man's place in the modern world. I shall limit myself to some extracts regarding sin and human sinfulness:

When man looks into his own heart, he finds that he is drawn toward what is wrong and sunk in many evils which cannot come from his good Creator. Often refusing to acknowledge God as his source, man has also upset the relationship which should link him to his last end; and at the same time he has broken the right order that should reign within himself as well as between himself and other men and all creatures. Man therefore is divided in himself. As a result, the whole life of men, both individual and social, shows itself to be a struggle, and a dramatic one, between good and evil, between light and darkness. Man finds that he is unable of himself to overcome the assaults of evil successfully, so that everyone feels as though bound by chains. But the Lord himself came to free and strengthen man, renewing him inwardly and casting out the 'prince of this world' (Jn 12:31), who held him in the bondage of sin. For sin brought man to a lower state, forcing him away from the completeness that is his to attain. Both the high calling and the deep misery men experience find their final explanation in the light of this Revelation.[4]

It is impossible, then, to speak of the

"limit imposed upon evil" without considering the ideas contained in the passage just quoted. God himself came to save us and to deliver us from evil, and this coming of God, this "Advent," which we celebrate in such a joyful way in the weeks preceding the Nativity of the Lord, is truly redemptive. It is impossible to think of the limit placed by God himself upon the various forms of evil without reference to the mystery of Redemption.

Could the mystery of Redemption be the response to that historical evil which, in different forms, continually recurs in human affairs? Is it also the response to the evil of our own day? It can seem that the evil of concentration camps, of gas chambers, of police cruelty, of total war, and of oppressive regimes — evil which, among other things, systematically contradicts the message of the Cross — it can seem, I say, that such evil is more powerful than any good. Yet if we look more closely at the history of those peoples and nations who have endured the trial of totalitarian systems and persecutions on account of faith, we discover that this is precisely where the victorious presence of Christ's Cross is most clearly revealed. Against such a dramatic background, that presence may be even more striking. To those who are subjected to systematic evil, there remains only Christ and his Cross as a source of spiritual self-defense, as a promise of victory. Did not the sacrifice of Maximilian Kolbe in the extermination camp at Auschwitz become a sign of victory over evil? And could not the same be said of Edith Stein — that great thinker from the school of Husserl — who perished in the gas chamber of Birkenau, thus sharing the destiny of many other sons and daughters of Israel? And besides these two figures, so often named together, how many others in that tragic history stand out among their fellow prisoners for the strength of the witness they bore to Christ crucified and risen!

The mystery of Christ's Redemption puts down deep roots in our lives. Modern life is a predominantly technological civilization, but here too the mystery leaves its efficacious mark, as the Second Vatican Council reminds us:

To the question of how this unhappy situation can be overcome, Christians reply that all these human activities, which are daily endangered by pride and inordinate self-love, must be purified and perfected by the Cross and

Resurrection of Christ. Redeemed by Christ and made a new creature by the Holy Spirit, man can, indeed he must, love the things of God's creation: it is from God that he has received them, and it is as flowing from God's hand that he looks upon them and reveres them. Man thanks his divine benefactor for all these things, he uses them and enjoys them in a spirit of poverty and freedom: thus he is brought to a true possession of the world, as having nothing yet possessing everything.[5]

It could be said that the whole of the constitution *Gaudium et Spes* is an exploration of the definition of the world with which the document begins:

Therefore the world the Council has in mind is the whole human family seen in the context of everything which envelops it: it is the world as the theater of human history, bearing the marks of its travail, its triumphs and failures, the world, which in the Christian vision has been created and is sustained by the love of its maker, which has been freed from the slavery of sin by Christ, who was crucified and rose again in order to break the stranglehold of the evil one, so that it might be fashioned anew according to God's design and brought to its fulfilment.[6]

The vital words — Cross, Resurrection, and Paschal Mystery — appear again and again throughout *Gaudium et Spes*. All three point to the same thing: Redemption. The world is redeemed by God. The scholastics used to speak of *status naturae redemptae* — the state of redeemed nature. Although the Council hardly uses the word "Redemption," it frequently invokes the idea. In the language of the Council, Redemption is understood as the culmination of the Paschal Mystery in the Resurrection. Was there a reason for this choice? When I became more familiar with Eastern theology, I understood better the important ecumenical character that lay behind this conciliar vision. The insistence on the Resurrection was an expression of the spirituality typical of the great Fathers of the Christian East. If Redemption marks the divine limit placed upon evil, it is for this reason only: because thereby evil is radically overcome by good, hate by love, death by resurrection.

5. The Mystery of Redemption

In the light of these reflections, one is impelled to seek a fuller explanation of the nature of Redemption. What exactly is Redemption in the context of the battle between good and evil in which man is caught up?

Sometimes the battle is expressed using the image of a pair of scales. In terms of this symbol, we could say that God, through the sacrifice of his Son on the Cross, placed that expiation of infinite value on the side of good, so that it would always ultimately prevail. In Polish, the word for "Redeemer" is *Odkupiciel,* derived from the verb *odkupić* meaning "regain." Similarly, the Latin term *Redemptor* is related to the verb *redimere* (regain). This etymological analysis may bring us closer to understanding the reality of the Redemption.

Closely connected to it are the concepts of forgiveness and justification. Both these terms belong to the language of the Gospel. Christ forgave sins, strongly emphasizing that the Son of Man had the power to do so. When they brought the paralytic before him, the first thing he said was: "My son, your sins are forgiven" (Mk 2:5); only later did he add: "Rise, take up your bed and go home" (Mk 2:11). In so doing he implicitly made the point that sin is a greater evil than physical paralysis. And after the Resurrection, when he appeared for the first time in the Upper Room where the Apostles were assembled, he showed them the wounds in his hands and his side, breathed on them, and said: "Receive the Holy Spirit. If you forgive the sins of any, they are forgiven; if you retain the sins of any, they are retained" (Jn 20: 22–23). In this way he revealed that the power to forgive sins, which only God possesses, has been given to the Church. At the same time he reaffirmed that sin is the greatest evil from which man has to be delivered, and he showed that the faculty to bring about this deliverance has been entrusted to the Church through the Passion and redemptive death of Christ.

Saint Paul expresses the same truth in greater depth through the concept of justification. In the Apostle's Letters — especially those to the Romans and the Galatians — the doctrine of justification even acquires a polemical connotation. Paul was formed in the schools of the Pharisees, who were well versed in the study of the Old Covenant, and he challenges their conviction that the Law was the source of justification. In reality, he affirms, man does not attain justification through the actions prescribed by the Law — particularly not through observing the multiple prescriptions of ritual character, to which great importance was then attached. Justification has its source in faith in Christ (cf. Gal 2:15–21). It is Christ crucified who justifies sinful man every time the latter, through his faith in the Redemption accomplished by Christ, repents of his sins, is converted, and returns to God as his Father. Hence, from one point of view, the concept of justification is an even deeper expression of the content of the mystery of Redemption. To be justified before God, human effort is not enough; the grace which pours forth from Christ's sacrifice is also needed. Only the immolation of Christ on the Cross has the power to restore man's righteousness before God.

The Resurrection of Christ clearly illustrates that only the measure of good introduced by God into history through the mystery of Redemption is sufficient to correspond fully to the truth of the human being. The Paschal Mystery thus becomes the definitive measure of man's existence in the world created by God. In this mystery, not only is eschatological truth revealed to us, that is to say the fullness of the Gospel, or Good News. There also shines forth a light to enlighten the whole of human existence in its temporal dimension and this light is then reflected onto the created world. Christ, through his Resurrection, has so to speak "justified" the work of creation, and especially the creation of man. He has "justified" it in the sense that he has revealed the "just measure" of good intended by God at the beginning of human history. This measure is not merely what was provided by him in creation and then compromised by man through sin; it is a superabundant measure, in which the original plan finds a higher realization (cf. Gn 3:14–15). In Christ, man is called to a new life, as son in the Son, the perfect expression of God's glory. In the words of Saint Irenaeus, *gloria Dei vivens homo* — the glory of God is man fully alive.[7]

6. Redemption: Victory Given as a Task to Man

Redemption, remission, and justification, then, are expressions of God's love and mercy toward us. What is the relationship between the mystery of Redemption and human freedom? In the light of Redemption, how do we find the path we must choose in order to realize fully our own freedom?

In the mystery of Redemption, Christ's victory over evil is given to us not simply for our personal advantage, but also as a task. We accept that task as we set out upon the way of the interior life, working consciously on ourselves — with Christ as our Teacher. The Gospel calls us to follow this very path. Christ's call "Follow me!" is echoed on many pages of the Gospel and is addressed to different people — not only to the Galilean fishermen whom Jesus calls to become his Apostles (cf. Mt 4:19, Mk 1:17, Jn 1:43), but also, for example, to the rich young man in the Synoptic Gospels (cf. Mt 19:16–22, Mk 10:17–22, Lk 18:18–23). Jesus's conversation with him is one of the key texts to which we must constantly return, from various points of view, as I did, for example, in the encyclical *Veritatis Splendor*.[8]

The call "Follow me!" is an invitation to set out along the path to which the inner dynamic of the mystery of Redemption leads us. This is the path indicated by the teaching, so often found in writings on the interior life and on mystical experience, about the three stages involved in "following Christ." These three stages are sometimes called "ways." We speak of the purgative way, the illuminative way, and the unitive way. In reality, these are not three distinct ways, but three aspects of the same way, along which Christ calls everyone, as he once called that young man in the Gospel.

When the young man asks: "Teacher, what good deed must I do to have eternal life?", Christ answers him: "If you wish to enter life, keep the commandments" (Mt 19:16–17 *et passim*). And when the young man continues to ask: "Which?" Christ simply reminds him of the principal commandments of the Decalogue, and especially those from the so-called "second tablet" concerning relations with one's neighbor. In Christ's teaching, of course, all the commandments are summarized in the commandment to love God above all things and one's neighbor as oneself. He says so explicitly to a doctor of the Law in response to a question (cf. Mt 22:34–40; Mk 12:28–31). Observance of the commandments, properly understood, is synonymous with the purgative way: it means conquering sin, moral evil in its various guises. And this leads to a gradual inner purification.

It also enables us to discover values. And hence we conclude that the purgative way leads organically into the illuminative way. Values are lights which illumine existence and, as we work on our lives, they shine ever more brightly on the horizon. So side by side with observance of the commandments — which has an essentially purgative meaning — we develop virtues. For example, in observing the commandment: "You shall not kill!" we discover the value of life under various aspects and we learn an ever deeper respect for it. In observing the commandment: "You shall not commit adultery!" we acquire the virtue of purity, and this means that we come to an ever greater awareness of the gratuitous beauty of the human body, of masculinity and femininity. This gratuitous beauty becomes a light for our actions. In observing the commandment: "You shall not bear false witness!" we learn the virtue of truthfulness. This not only excludes all lying and hypocrisy from our lives, but it develops within us a kind of "instinct for truth" which guides all our actions. And living thus in the truth, we acquire in our own humanity a connatural truthfulness.

So the illuminative stage in the interior life emerges gradually from the purgative stage. With the passage of time, if we persevere in following Christ our Teacher, we feel less and less burdened by the struggle against sin, and we enjoy more and more the divine light which pervades all creation. This is most important, because it allows us to escape from a situation of constant inner exposure to the risk of sin — even though, on this earth, the risk always remains present to some degree — so as to move with ever greater freedom within the whole of the created world. This same freedom and simplicity characterizes our relations with other human beings, including those of the opposite sex. Interior light illumines our actions and shows us all the good in the created world as coming from the hand of God. Thus the purgative way and then the illuminative way form the organic introduction to what is known as the unitive way.

This is the final stage of the interior journey, when the soul experiences a special union with God. This union is realized in contemplation of the divine Being and in the experience of love which flows from it with growing intensity. In this way we somehow anticipate what is destined to be ours in eternity, beyond death and the grave. Christ, supreme Teacher of the spiritual life, together with all those who have been formed in his school, teaches that even in this life we can enter onto the path of union with God.

The dogmatic constitution *Lumen Gentium* states: "Christ, made obedient unto death and because of this exalted by the Father (cf. Phil 2:8–9), has entered into the glory of his kingdom. All things are subjected to him until he subjects himself and all created things to the Father, so that God may be all in all (cf. 1 Cor 15:27–28)."[9] Evidently the Council is thinking on a very large scale, illustrating what it means to participate in Christ's kingly mission. At the same time, however, these words help us to understand how union with God can be achieved during earthly life. If the kingly way, indicated by Christ, leads definitively to the state in which "God will be all in all," the union with God that can be experienced on earth is attained in just the same way. We can find God in everything, we can commune with him in and through all things. Created things cease to be a danger for us as once they were, particularly while we were still at the purgative stage of our journey. Creation, and other people in particular, not only regain their true light, given to them by God the Creator, but, so to speak, they lead us to God himself, in the way that he willed to reveal himself to us: as Father, Redeemer, and Spouse.

FREEDOM
AND RESPONSIBILITY

7. Toward a Just Use of Freedom

After the fall of the totalitarian systems in which human enslavement reached its apex, the prospect of freedom opened up for the oppressed citizens — the possibility, in other words, of deciding for themselves and by themselves. Many opinions have been expressed on this matter. The fundamental question could be formulated as follows: How can these possibilities of free decision best be used so as to avoid any future return of the evil at work in those systems and those ideologies?

If those societies sensed a new freedom after the collapse of the totalitarian systems, a fundamental new problem arose almost immediately — the proper use of that freedom. The problem affects both individuals and societies: it therefore requires some kind of systematic solution. If I am free, I can make good or bad use of my freedom. If I use it well, I in my turn become more "good" as a result, and the good I have accomplished has a positive influence on those around me. If on the other hand I use it wrongly, evil will take root and begin to spread both in me and around me. The danger of the situation in which we live today consists in the fact that we claim to prescind from the ethical dimension in our use of freedom — that is, from consideration of moral good and evil. A certain concept of freedom, which has widespread support in public opinion at present, diverts attention from ethical responsibilities. Appeal is made today to freedom alone. It is often said: what matters is to be free, released from all constraint or limitation, so as to operate according to private judgment, which in reality is often pure caprice. This much is clear: such liberalism can only be described as primitive. Its influence, however, is potentially devastating.

We should add immediately that European traditions, especially those of the Enlightenment period, have recognized the need for a criterion to regulate the use of freedom. Yet the criterion adopted has been not so much that of the just good (*bonum honestum*) as that of utility or pleasure. Here we are faced with a most important element in the tradition of European thought, one to which we must now devote a little more attention.

In human action, the different spiritual faculties tend toward a synthesis in which the leading role is played by the will. The subject thus imprints his own rationality upon his actions. Human acts are free and, as such, they engage the responsibility of the subject. Man wants a particular good and he chooses it: he is consequently responsible for his choice.

Against the background of this vision of good, which is both metaphysical and anthropological, there arises a distinction of properly ethical character. It is the distinction between the just good (*bonum honestum*), the useful good (*bonum utile*), and the pleasurable good (*bonum delectabile*). These three types of good are intimately bound up with human action. When he acts, man chooses a certain good, which becomes the goal of his action. If the subject chooses a *bonum honestum,* his goal is conformed to the very essence of the object of his action and is therefore a just goal. When on the other hand the object of his choice is a *bonum utile,* the goal is the advantage to be gained from it for the subject. The question of the morality of the action remains open: only when the action bringing the advantage is just and the means used are just, can the subject's goal also be said to be just. It is precisely on this issue that a rift begins to emerge between the Aristotelian-Thomistic ethical tradition and modern utilitarianism.

Utilitarianism ignores the first and fundamental dimension of good, that of the *bonum honestum*. Utilitarian anthropology and the ethic derived from it set out from the conviction that man tends essentially toward his own interest or that of the group to which he belongs. Ultimately, the aim of human action is personal or corporate advantage. As for the *bonum delectabile,* it is of course taken into account in the Aristotelian-Thomistic tradition. The great exponents of this current of thought, in their ethical reflection, are fully aware that the accomplishment of a just good is always accompanied by an interior joy — the joy of the good. In utilitarian thought, however, the dimension of good and the dimension of joy have been displaced by the search for advantage or pleasure. In this scheme, the *bonum delectabile* of Thomistic thought has been somehow emancipated, becoming both a good and an end in itself. In the utilitarian vision, man in acting seeks pleasure above all else, not the *honestum*. Admittedly, utilitarians like Jeremy Bentham or

John Stuart Mill emphasize that the goal is not simply pleasure at sense level: spiritual pleasures also come into play. They say that these too must be considered in making the so-called "calculation of pleasures." It is this calculation which, to their way of thinking, constitutes the "normative" expression of the utilitarian ethic: the greatest happiness of the greatest number. All human action, individually and jointly, has to conform to this principle.

One response to the utilitarian ethic was offered by the philosophy of Immanuel Kant. The Königsberg philosopher rightly observed that giving priority to pleasure in the analysis of human action is dangerous and threatens the very essence of morality. In his aprioristic vision of reality, Kant places two things in question, namely pleasure and expediency. Yet he does not return to the tradition of the *bonum honestum*. Instead he bases all human morality on aprioristic forms of the practical intellect, which have imperative character. Essential for morals is the categorical imperative which, for Kant, is expressed in the following formula: "Act only according to a maxim by which you can at the same time will that it shall become a universal law."[10]

Then there is a second form of categorical

imperative, in which the person is given due priority in the moral order. This is the formulation: "Act in such a way that you always treat humanity, whether in your own person or in the person of any other, never simply as a means, but always at the same time as an end."[11] In this form, the end and the means reappear in Kant's ethical thought, but as secondary rather than primary categories. The primary category becomes the person. Kant could be said to have laid the foundations of modern personalist ethics. From the point of view of the development of ethical reflection, this is a very important step. The Neo-Thomists also took up the personalist principle, basing themselves on Saint Thomas's concept of the *bonum honestum, bonum utile, bonum delectabile*.

It is clear from this synthetic presentation that the question of the just use of freedom is closely linked with reflection on the topic of good and evil. It is a pressing question from both a practical and a theoretical point of view. If ethics is the branch of philosophy concerned with moral good and evil, then it has to draw its fundamental criterion of evaluation from the essential property of the human will, in other words, freedom. Man can do good or evil because his will is free, but also fallible. Whenever he makes a choice, he does so in the light of a criterion which may be objective goodness or may be utilitarian advantage. With the ethics of the categorical imperative, Kant rightly emphasized the obligatory character of man's moral choices. At the same time, however, he distanced himself from the only truly objective criterion for those choices: he underlined the subjective obligation but overlooked what lies at the foundation of morals, that is the *bonum honestum.* As for the *bonum delectabile,* in the sense in which it is understood by the Anglo-Saxon utilitarians, Kant essentially excluded it from the realm of morals.

The whole of the argument developed thus far concerning the theory of good and evil belongs to moral philosophy. I devoted some years of work to these problems at the Catholic University of Lublin. I put together my ideas on the subject firstly in the book *Love and Responsibility,* then in *The Acting Person,* and finally in the Wednesday catecheses which were published under the title *"Original Unity of Man and Woman."* On the basis of further reading and research undertaken during the ethics seminar at Lublin, I came to see how important these problems were for a number of contemporary thinkers: Max Scheler and other phenomenologists, Jean-Paul Sartre, Emmanuel Levinas, and Paul Ricœur, but also Vladimir Soloviev, not to mention Fyodor Dostoyevsky. Through these analyses of anthropological reality, various manifestations emerge of man's desire for Redemption, and confirmation is given of the need for a Redeemer if man is to attain salvation.

8. Freedom Is for Love

Recent history has provided ample and tragically eloquent evidence of the evil use of freedom. Yet a positive answer still needs to be given to the underlying question: What does freedom consist of and what purpose does it serve?

Here we are addressing a problem which, if it has always been important in the past, has become even more so since the events of 1989. What is human freedom? The answer can be traced back to Aristotle. Freedom, for Aristotle, is a property of the will which is realized through truth. It is given to man as a task to be accomplished. There is no freedom without truth. Freedom is an ethical category. Aristotle teaches this principally in his *Nicomachean Ethics*, constructed on the basis of rational truth. This natural ethic was adopted in its entirety by Saint Thomas in his *Summa Theologiae*. So it was that the *Nicomachean Ethics* remained a significant influence in the history of morals, having now taken on the characteristics of a Christian Thomistic ethic.

Saint Thomas embraced the entire Aristotelian system of virtues. The good that is to be accomplished by human freedom is precisely the good of the virtues. Most of all, this refers to the four so-called cardinal virtues: prudence, justice, fortitude, and temperance. Prudence has a guiding function. Justice regulates social order. Temperance and fortitude, on the other hand, discipline man's inner life, that is to say, they determine the good in relation to human irascibility and concupiscence: *vis irascibilis* and *vis concupiscibilis*. Hence, the *Nicomachean Ethics* are clearly based upon a genuine anthropology.

The other virtues take their place within the system of the cardinal virtues, subordinated to them in different ways. This system, on which the self-realization of human freedom in truth depends, can be described as exhaustive. It is not an abstract or *a priori* system. Aristotle sets out from the experience of the moral subject. Likewise, Saint Thomas finds his starting point in moral experience, but through this he also seeks the light that is offered by Sacred Scripture. The greatest light comes from the commandment to love God and neighbor. In this commandment, human freedom finds its most complete realization. Freedom is for love: its realization through love can even reach heroic proportions. Christ speaks of "laying down his life" for his friends, for other human beings. In the history of Christianity, many people in different ways have "laid down their lives" for their neighbor, and they have done so in order to follow the example of Christ. This is particularly true in the case of martyrs, whose testimony has accompanied Christianity from apostolic times right up to the present day. The twentieth century was the great century of Christian martyrs, and this is true both in the Catholic Church and in other Churches and ecclesial communities.

Returning to Aristotle, we should add that, as well as the *Nicomachean Ethics*, he also left us a work on social ethics. It is entitled *Politics*. Here, without addressing questions concerning the concrete strategies of political life, Aristotle limits himself to defining the ethical principles on which any just political system should be based. Catholic social teaching owes much to Aristotle's *Politics* and has acquired particular prominence in modern times, thanks to the issue of labor. After Leo XIII's great 1891 encyclical, *Rerum Novarum*, the twentieth century saw several more magisterial documents, of vital importance for the many issues that gradually surfaced in the social arena. Pius XI's encyclical *Quadragesimo anno*, marking the fortieth anniversary of *Rerum Novarum*, directly addresses the labor issue. In *Mater et Magistra*, John XXIII, for his part, offers an in-depth discussion of social justice with reference to the vast sector of agricultural labor; later, in the encyclical *Pacem in Terris*, he sets out the ground rules for a just peace and a new international order, resuming and further exploring certain principles already contained in some important statements by Pius XII. Paul VI, in his apostolic letter *Octogesima Adveniens*, returns to the issue of industrial labor, while his encyclical *Populorum Progressio* analyzes the various elements of just development. All these issues were proposed for the reflection of the Fathers of the Second Vatican Council, and they received particular attention in the constitution *Gaudium et Spes*. Setting out from the fundamental notion of the human person's vocation, this conciliar document analyzes one by one the many different dimensions of this vocation. In particular, it dwells on marriage and the family, it considers cultural issues, and it addresses complex questions of economic, political, and social life both nationally and internationally. I myself returned to the last of these issues in two encyclicals, *Sollicitudo Rei Socialis* and *Centesimus Annus*. Yet earlier still, I had devoted a whole encyclical to human labor, *Laborem Exercens*. This document, intended to mark the ninetieth anniversary of *Rerum Novarum*, was published late because of the attempt on my life.

At the heart of all these magisterial documents lies the theme of human freedom. Freedom is given to man by the Creator as a gift and at the same time as a task. Through freedom, man is called to accept and to implement the truth regarding the good. In choosing and bringing about a genuine good in personal and family life, in the economic and political sphere, in national and international arenas, man brings about his own freedom in the truth. This allows him to escape or to overcome possible deviations recorded by history. One of these was certainly Renaissance Machiavellianism. Others include various forms of social utilitarianism, based on class (Marxism) or nationalism (national socialism, fascism). Once these two systems had fallen in Europe, the societies affected, especially in the former Soviet bloc, faced the problem of liberalism. This was treated at length in the encyclical *Centesimus Annus* and, from another angle, in the encyclical *Veritatis Splendor*. In these debates the age-old questions return, which had already been treated at the end of the nineteenth century by Leo XIII, who devoted a number of encyclicals to the issue of freedom.

From this rapid outline of the history of thought on this topic, it is clear that the issue of human freedom is fundamental. Freedom is properly so called to the extent that it implements the truth regarding the good. Only then does it become a good in itself. If freedom ceases to be linked with truth and begins to make truth dependent on freedom, it sets the premises for dangerous moral consequences, which can assume incalculable dimensions. When this happens, the abuse of freedom provokes a reaction which takes the form of one totalitarian system or another. This is another form of the corruption of freedom, the consequences of which we have experienced in the twentieth century, and beyond.

9. The Lessons of Recent History

Holy Father, you were a firsthand witness of a long and difficult period in the history of Poland and other former Eastern-bloc countries (1939–1989). What lessons do you think can be learned from the experience of your native country and, in particular, from what the Polish Church experienced during that period?

The fifty-year struggle against totalitarianism was not without a certain providential significance: in those years, a widespread need was expressed for self-defense against the enslavement of an entire population. This should not be understood in purely negative terms. Not only did the people reject nazism as a system aimed at the destruction of Poland, and communism as an oppressive system imposed from the East, but in the process of resistance they also pursued highly positive ideals. More was involved than a simple rejection of these hostile systems. Those same years saw the

71

recovery and the strengthening of the fundamental values by which the people lived and to which they wished to remain faithful. I am referring here both to the relatively brief period of German occupation and to the forty years and more of Communist domination, during the People's Republic of Poland.

Was this process fully conscious? Was it to some degree instinctive? In many instances it probably was instinctive to a greater or lesser degree. In their resistance to the regime, the Poles were not so much making a choice based on theoretical arguments, it was more the case that they could not do other than resist. It was a matter of instinct or intuition, although at the same time it prompted a deeper reflection on the religious and civil values motivating their resistance, to a degree previously unknown in Polish history.

Here I should like to refer to a conversation I had during my studies in Rome with one of my college companions, a young Flemish priest. He was associated with the work of Fr. Joseph Cardijn, the future Cardinal, namely the so-called JOC (YCW), or *Jeunesse Ouvrière Chrétienne* (Young Christian Workers). The topic of our conversation was the situation in Europe after the Second World War. My colleague expressed himself more or less as follows: "The Lord allowed the experience of such an evil as communism to affect you . . . And why did he allow it?" His answer to this question I find significant: "We were spared this in the West, because perhaps we could not have withstood so great a trial. You, on the other hand, can take it." This remark by the young Fleming remained fixed in my memory. To some degree it had a prophetic value. I often recall it and I see ever more clearly the accuracy of his diagnosis.

Naturally, it would be wrong to overstate the element of dichotomy in a Europe divided between East and West. The countries of Western Europe have a more ancient Christian tradition. They have witnessed the highest accomplishments of Christian culture. In Western Europe, the Church has been blessed with a multitude of saints. There have been stupendous works of art: the majestic Romanesque and Gothic cathedrals, the baroque basilicas, the paintings of Giotto, Fra Angelico, and the countless artists of the fifteenth and sixteenth centuries, the sculptures of Michelangelo, the dome of Saint Peter's, and the Sistine Chapel. It was here that the *Summae Theologiae* came to birth, foremost among them that of Saint Thomas Aquinas; here were formed the highest traditions of Christian spirituality, the works of the German mystics, the writings of Saint Catherine of Siena in Italy, of Saint Teresa of Avila, and Saint John of the Cross in Spain. Here the great monastic orders were born, beginning with that of Saint Benedict, who is rightly called the father and teacher of Europe; here too the worthy mendicant orders, including the Franciscans and the Dominicans, and also the congregations of the Counter-Reformation and subsequent centuries, which have done and continue to do so much good work. The Church's great missionary endeavor drew its resources principally from Western Europe, and in our own day wonderful, dynamic apostolic movements are emerging there, whose witness cannot fail to bear fruit in the temporal order. In this sense we may say that Christ is always the "cornerstone" of the building and the rebuilding of society in the Christian West.

At the same time, however, we cannot ignore the insistent return of the denial of Christ. Again and again we encounter the signs of an alternative civilization to that built on Christ as "cornerstone" — a civilization which, even if not explicitly atheist, is at least positivistic and agnostic, since it is built upon the principle of thinking and acting as if God did not exist. This approach can easily be recognized in the modern so-called scientific, or rather scientistic, mentality, and it can be recognized in literature, especially the mass media. To live as if God did not exist means to live outside the parameters of good and evil, outside the context of values derived from God. It is claimed that man himself can decide what is good or bad. And this program is widely promoted in all sorts of ways.

If, on the one hand, the West continues to provide evidence of zealous evangelization, on the other hand anti-evangelical currents are equally strong. They strike at the very foundations of human morality, influencing the family and promoting a morally permissive outlook: divorce, free love, abortion, contraconception, the fight against life in its initial phases and in its final phase, the manipulation of life. This program is supported by enormous financial resources, not only in individual countries, but also on a worldwide scale. It has great centers of economic power at its disposal, through which it attempts to impose its own conditions on developing countries. Faced with all this, one may legitimately ask whether this is not another form of totalitarianism, subtly concealed under the appearances of democracy.

Maybe all this was what my Flemish companion had in mind when he suggested that the West "could not have withstood so great a trial," and then added "You, on the other hand, can take it." It is significant that after I became Pope, I heard the same opinion expressed by an eminent European politician. He said to me: "If Soviet communism comes to the West, we will not be able to defend ourselves . . . There is no force strong enough to mobilize us for such a defense . . ." We know that communism fell in the end because of the system's socioeconomic weakness, not because it has been truly rejected as an ideology or a philosophy. In certain quarters in the West, there are still those who regret its passing.

What lessons can we learn from those years dominated by "ideologies of evil" and the struggle against them? Firstly, I think we must learn to go to the roots. Only then can the harm done by fascism or communism somehow enrich us and lead us toward good, which is undoubtedly the proper Christian response. "Do not be overcome by evil, but overcome evil with good" (Rom 12:21), writes Saint Paul. From this point of view, we in Poland have a contribution to make. This will happen if we learn to go beneath the surface, without yielding to the propaganda of the Enlightenment. We managed to resist this in the eighteenth century, and thereby in the course of the nineteenth century we were able to acquire the determination necessary to regain independence after the First World War. The fiber of the population was revealed once again in the struggle against communism, which Poland was able to resist until the victory of 1989. We must not let those sacrifices prove to have been in vain.

At the Congress of theologians of Central and Eastern Europe held at Lublin in 1991, an attempt was made to sum up the experience of the Churches during that time of struggle against Communist totalitarianism, and to testify to it. The theology developed in that part of Europe is different from Western theology. It is something more than theology in the strict sense. It is testimony of life, testimony of what it means to place oneself in God's hands, to "learn Christ," who entrusted himself into the Father's hands to the point where he cried out from the Cross: "Father, into your hands I commend my spirit" (Lk 23:46). This is what "learning Christ" means: penetrating the depths of the mystery of God, who in this way brings about the Redemption of the world. I met the participants in that Congress during my pilgrimage to Jasna Góra, on the occasion of the World Youth Day, and later I was able to read many of the papers they had presented: these documents can be upsetting in their simplicity and their profundity.

In trying to speak of these matters we encounter a serious difficulty. They are so varied and complex that they often verge on the inexpressible. In all this, however, we glimpse the action of God, manifested through human mediation: both in the good that men do, and also in their errors, from which he is able to draw forth a greater good. The entire twentieth century was marked by a singular intervention of God, the Father who is "rich in mercy" — *dives in misericordia* (Eph 2:4).

10. The Mystery of Mercy

Holy Father, could we dwell for a moment on the mystery of love and mercy? It seems important to analyze in greater depth the essence of these two divine attributes of such significance for us.

The psalm *Miserere* is possibly one of the most beautiful prayers that the Church inherited from the Old Testament. The circumstances of its origin are well known. It was born as the cry of a sinner, King David, who took for himself the wife of the soldier Uriah, committed adultery with her, and then, in order to conceal the traces of his crime, arranged for her rightful husband to die on the battlefield. In a striking passage from the Second Book of Samuel, the prophet Nathan points an accusing finger at David, declaring him responsible for a great crime before God: "You are the man!" (2 Sam 12:7). The king experiences a kind of revelation, and is overcome with profound emotion which finds expression in the words of the *Miserere*. This psalm probably occurs more often in the liturgy than any other:

Miserere mei, Deus,
secundum misericordiam tuam;
et secundum multitudinem
*   miserationum tuarum*
dele iniquitatem meam.

Amplius lava me ab iniquitate mea,
et a peccato meo munda me.
Quoniam iniquitatem meam ego
*   cognosco,*
et peccatum meum contra me est
*   semper.*

Tibi, tibi soli peccavi
et malum coram te feci,
ut iustus inveniaris in sententia tua
et aequus in iudicio tuo . . .

There is a particular beauty in these gently flowing Latin words and in the gradual unfolding of thoughts, feelings, and emotions. Clearly the original language of the psalm *Miserere* was different, but our ear is accustomed to the Latin version, perhaps more than to the vernacular translations, although these too are melodious and evocative in their own way:

> Have mercy on me, O God, in your
>   kindness,
> In your compassion blot out my
>   offense.
> O wash me more and more from
>   my guilt,
> and cleanse me from my sin.

> My offenses truly I know them;
> my sin is always before me.
> Against you, you alone, have I
>   sinned,
> what is evil in your sight I have
>   done.

> That you may be justified when
>   you give sentence,
> and be without reproach when you
>   judge,
> O see, in guilt I was born,
> a sinner was I conceived.

> Indeed you love truth in the heart;
> then in the secret of my heart teach
>   me wisdom.
> O purify me, then I shall be clean;
> O wash me, I shall be whiter than
>   snow.

Make me hear rejoicing and
    gladness,
that the bones you have crushed
    may revive.
From my sins turn away your face
and blot out all my guilt.

A pure heart create for me, O God,
put a steadfast spirit within me.
Do not cast me away from your
    presence
nor deprive me of your holy spirit.

Give me again the joy of your help;
with a spirit of fervor sustain me,
that I may teach transgressors your
    ways
and sinners may return to you.

O rescue me, God, my helper,
and my tongue shall ring out your
    goodness.
O Lord, open my lips
and my mouth shall declare your
    praise.
      (Ps(s) 50/51:3–17)[12]

These verses require practically no comment. They speak for themselves, revealing the truth about man's moral fragility. He accuses himself before God because he knows that sin contradicts the holiness of his Creator. At the same time, sinful man knows that God is infinite mercy, always ready to forgive and to restore the sinner to righteousness.

Where does the Father's infinite mercy come from? David is a man of the Old Covenant. He knows the One God. We, as people of the New Covenant, are able to recognize in the Davidic *Miserere* the voice of Christ, the Son of God, treated by the Father as sin for our sake (cf. 2 Cor 5:21). Christ took upon himself the sins of us all (cf. Is 53:12), so as to make satisfaction for justice wounded by sin; in this way he maintained a balance between the justice and the mercy of the Father. It is significant that Sister Faustina saw this Son as the merciful God, yet she contemplated him not so much on the Cross but rather in his subsequent state of risen glory. She thus linked her mystical sense of mercy with the mystery of Easter, in which Christ appears triumphant over sin and death (cf. Jn 20:19–23).

I have chosen here to speak of Sister Faustina and the devotion to the merciful Christ which she promoted, because she too belongs to our time. She lived in the first decades of the twentieth century and died before the Second World War. In that very period the mystery of Divine Mercy was revealed to her, and what she experienced she then recorded in her *Diary*. To those who survived the Second World War, Saint Faustina's *Diary* appears as a particular Gospel of Divine Mercy, written from a twentieth-century perspective. The people of that time understood her message. They understood it in the light of the dramatic buildup of evil during the Second World War and the cruelty of the totalitarian systems. It was as if Christ had wanted to reveal that the limit imposed upon evil, of which man is both perpetrator and victim, is ultimately Divine Mercy. Of course, there is also justice, but this alone does not have the last word in the divine economy of world history and human history. God can always draw good from evil, he wills that all should be saved and come to knowledge of the truth (cf. 1 Tim 2:4): God is Love (cf. 1 Jn 4:8). Christ, crucified and risen, just as he appeared to Sister Faustina, is the supreme revelation of this truth.

Here I should like to return to what I said about the experience of the Church in Poland during the period of resistance to communism. It seems to me to have a universal value. I think that the same applies to

Sister Faustina and her witness to the mystery of Divine Mercy. The patrimony of her spirituality was of great importance, as we know from experience, for the resistance against the evil and inhuman systems of the time. The lesson to be drawn from all this is important not only for the Poles, but also in every part of the world where the Church is present. This became clear during the beatification and canonization of Sister Faustina. It was as if Christ had wanted to say through her: "Evil does not have the last word!" The Paschal Mystery confirms that good is ultimately victorious, that life conquers death and that love triumphs over hate.

THINKING "MY COUNTRY"

(NATIVE LAND — NATION — STATE)

11. On the Concept of *Patria* (Native Land)

After the eruption of evil and the two great wars of the twentieth century, the world is turning into an increasingly interdependent group of continents, states, and societies; at the same time, Europe — or at least a considerable part of it — is tending toward not only economic but also political union. Indeed, the range of issues for which the agencies of the European Community have competence includes much more than just economics and ordinary politics. The fall of the totalitarian systems in neighboring countries made it possible for Poland to regain its independence and its openness toward the West. At present we need to redefine Poland's relationship with Europe and with the rest of the world. Until a short time ago there was much discussion of the consequences — profits and costs — of entry into the European Union. There was particular concern that the nation might lose its culture and the

State its sovereignty. Poland's entry into a larger community makes us reflect on the possible consequences for a particular cause that has been highly valued in Polish history: patriotism. Sustained by this sentiment, many Poles through the centuries have been prepared to give their lives in the struggle for the freedom of their native land, and many have indeed made that supreme sacrifice.

What in your view, Holy Father, is the meaning of the concepts of "native land," "nation," "culture"? How are they related to one another?

The Latin word *patria* is associated with the idea and the reality of "father" (*pater*). The native land (or fatherland) can in some ways be identified with patrimony — that is, the totality of goods bequeathed to us by our forefathers. In this context it is significant that one frequently hears the expression "motherland." Through personal experience we all know to what extent the transmission of our spiritual patrimony takes place through our mothers. Our native land is thus our heritage and it is also the whole patrimony derived from that heritage. It refers to the land, the territory, but more importantly, the concept of patria includes the values and the spiritual content that make up the culture of a given nation. I spoke about this very matter to UNESCO on June 2, 1980, pointing out that even when the Poles were deprived of their territory and the nation was partitioned, they maintained their sense of spiritual patrimony, the culture received from their forebears. Indeed, this sense developed in them in an extraordinarily dynamic way.

It is well known that the nineteenth century marked a high point in Polish culture. Never before had the Polish nation produced writers of such genius as Adam Mickiewicz, Juliusz Słowacki, Zygmunt Krasiński, Cyprian Norwid. Polish music had never before reached such heights as in the works of Fryderyk Chopin, Stanisław Moniuszko, and other composers, through whom the artistic patrimony of the nineteenth century was enriched for future generations. The same can be said of the plastic arts, painting and sculpture. The nineteenth century is the century of Jan Matejko and Artur Grottger; at the turn of the twentieth century Stanisław Wyspiański appears on the scene, an extraordinary genius in several fields, followed by Jacek Malczewski and others. What of Polish theater? The nineteenth century was a pioneering century for theatrical art: at the beginning we find the great Wojciech Bogusławski, whose artistic teaching was received and developed by numerous others, especially in Southern Poland, in Kraków and in Lviv, which was then part of Poland. The theater was living through its golden age, both in serious drama and in popular theater. It must be said that this same period of extraordinary cultural maturity during the nineteenth century fortified the Poles for the great struggle which led the nation to regain its independence. Poland, having been struck off the map of Europe, reappeared in 1918 and has remained there ever since. Not even the insane storm of hate unleashed from East and West between 1939 and 1945 could destroy it.

From this it can be seen that the very idea of "native land" presupposes a deep bond between the spiritual and the material, between culture and territory. Territory seized by force from a nation somehow becomes a plea crying out to the "spirit" of the nation itself. The spirit of the nation awakens, takes on fresh vitality, and struggles to restore the rights of the land. Norwid expressed all this concisely, in a reference to work: "Beauty is to enthuse us for work, and work is to raise us up."[13]

Now that we have begun our analysis of the concept of "native land," we do well to turn to the Gospel. Here, on the lips of Jesus, the word "Father" is fundamental. In fact, it is the name he uses most often. "All things have been delivered to me by my Father" (Mt 11:27; Lk 10:22); "the Father loves the Son, and shows him all that he himself is doing; and greater works than these will he show him" (Jn 5:20; cf. also Jn 5:21ff.). Christ's teachings contain the most profound elements of a theological vision of both native land and culture. Christ, as the Son who has come to us from the Father, presents himself to humanity with a particular patrimony, a particular heritage. Saint Paul speaks of this in the Letter to the Galatians: "When the time had fully come, God sent forth his Son, born of woman . . . so that we might receive adoption as sons . . . So through God you are no longer a slave, but a son; and if a son then an heir" (Gal 4:4–7).

Christ says: "I came from the Father and have come into the world" (Jn 16:28). This coming took place via a woman, his mother. The heritage of the eternal Father truly passed through Mary's heart and was thus enriched by all that the extraordinary feminine genius of the mother could bring to Christ's patrimony. In its universal dimension, Christianity is this patrimony, in which the mother's contribution is highly significant. This is why the Church is called mother: *mater Ecclesia*. In using this expression, we refer implicitly to the divine patrimony that we share, thanks to the coming of Christ.

So the Gospel gave a new meaning to the concept of native land. In its original sense, it means what we have inherited from our fathers and mothers on earth. The inheritance we receive from Christ orientates the patrimony of human native lands and cultures toward the eternal homeland. Christ says: "I came from the Father and have come into the world; again I am leaving the world and going to the Father" (Jn 16:28). Christ's departure to go to the Father introduces a new homeland into human history. Sometimes we speak of the "heavenly home," or "eternal home." These expressions indicate what has been accomplished in the history of man and the history of nations through Christ's coming into the world and through his leaving this world to go to the Father.

Christ's departure opened up the concept of native land to an eternal, eschatological dimension, but took nothing away from its temporal content. We know from experience, from the example of Polish history, how much the thought of the eternal homeland can inspire people to serve their earthly native land, motivating citizens to accept all manner of sacrifices for it — often to a heroic degree. The saints raised by the Church to the honor of the altars in the course of history, especially in recent centuries, provide eloquent proof of this.

The native land as patrimony comes from God, but to some extent it also comes from the world. Christ came into the world to confirm the eternal laws of God, the Creator. At the same time, however, he initiated an entirely new culture. Culture signifies cultivation. By his teaching, and by his life, death, and resurrection, Christ in some sense "recultivated" the world that the Father had created. Men and women became "God's field," as Saint Paul writes (cf. 1 Cor 3:9). In this way, the divine patrimony took on the form of "Christian culture." This is found not only in Christian societies and nations, but it has also somehow made its mark in the culture of all humanity. To some extent it has transformed that culture.

These reflections on the theme of the

native land help us to explore more deeply the meaning of the so-called Christian roots of Polish culture, and indeed of European culture more generally. When we use this expression, we normally think of the culture's historical roots, and with good reason, since culture has a historical character. The study of these roots, therefore, goes hand in hand with that of our history, including our political history. The efforts of the first Piast rulers,[14] intended to strengthen the Polish spirit through the establishment of a State on a defined European territory, were sustained by a particular spiritual inspiration. An expression of this was the baptism of Mieszko I and his people (966) at the instigation of his wife, the Bohemian Princess Dubravka. The influence this had upon the cultural orientation of that Slav nation on the banks of the Vistula is well known. Those Slav peoples who received the Christian message via Rus,[15] evangelized from Constantinople, received a different orientation. This distinction within the family of Slav nations lasts right up to the present, marking the spiritual boundaries of native lands and cultures.

12. Patriotism

A further question arises from these reflections on the concept of patria: How are we to understand patriotism in the light of the preceding discussion?

The preceding explanation of the concept of patria and its link with paternity and with generation points toward the moral value of patriotism. If we ask where patriotism appears in the Decalogue, the reply comes without hesitation: it is covered by the fourth commandment, which obliges us to honor our father and mother. It is included under the umbrella of the Latin word *pietas,* which underlines the religious dimension of the respect and veneration due to parents. We must venerate our parents, because for us they represent God the Creator. In giving us life, they share in the mystery of creation and therefore deserve a veneration related to that which we give to God the Creator. Patriotism includes this sentiment inasmuch as the patria truly resembles a mother. The spiritual patrimony which we acquire from our native land comes to us through our mother and father, and provides the basis for our corresponding duty of pietas.

Patriotism is a love for everything to do with our native land: its history, its traditions, its language, its natural features. It is a love which extends also to the works of our compatriots and the fruits of their genius. Every danger that threatens the overall good of our native land becomes an occasion to demonstrate this love. Our history teaches us that Poles have always been willing to make great sacrifices to preserve this good, or to regain it. The many tombs of soldiers who fought for Poland on different fronts around the world testify to this: they are widely dispersed, both at home and abroad. Yet I believe that the same could be said of every country and every nation in Europe and throughout the world.

The native land is the common good of all citizens and as such it imposes a serious duty. History amply documents the often heroic courage with which Poles have carried out this duty, when it was a question of defending the greater good of their native land. This is not to deny that some periods have witnessed a decline in this readiness to accept sacrifice in order to promote values and ideals connected with the notion of native land. At such times private interest and traditional Polish individualism have intervened as disruptive factors.

The native land, then, is a complex reality, in the service of which social structures have evolved and continue to evolve, starting from primitive tribal traditions. The question arises whether this evolution of human society has reached its final goal. Did not the twentieth century witness a widespread tendency to move toward supranational structures, even internationalism? And does this tendency not prove that small nations, in order to survive, have to allow themselves to be absorbed into larger political structures? These are legitimate questions. Yet it still seems that nation and native land, like the family, are permanent realities. In this regard, Catholic social doctrine speaks of "natural" societies, indicating that both the family and the nation have a particular bond with human nature, which has a social dimension. Every society's formation takes place in and through the family: of this there can be no doubt. Yet something similar could also be said about the nation. The cultural and historical identity of any society is preserved and nourished by all that is contained within this concept of nation. Clearly, one thing must be avoided at all costs: the risk of allowing this essential function of the nation to lead to an unhealthy nationalism. Of this, the twentieth century has supplied some all-too-eloquent examples, with disastrous consequences. How can we be delivered from such a danger? I think the right way is through patriotism. Whereas nationalism involves recognizing and pursuing the good of one's own nation alone, without regard for the rights of others, patriotism, on the other hand, is a love for one's native land that accords rights to all other nations equal to those claimed for one's own. Patriotism, in other words, leads to a properly ordered social love.

13. The Concept of Nation

Patriotism, as a sense of attachment to the nation and the native land, must not be allowed to degenerate into nationalism. Its proper interpretation depends on what we wish to express through the concept of nation. How, then, are we to understand the nation, this ideal entity to which patriotic sentiment refers?

If we examine the two terms carefully, we discover a close link between the meaning of *patria* (native land) and nation. In Polish, in fact — but not only in that language — the term *na-ród* (nation) comes from *ród* (generation); patria (*ojczy-zna*), however, has its root in the term father (*ojciec*). The father is the one who, together with the mother, gives life to a new human being. This "generation" by the father and mother is connected with patrimony, a concept underpinning the notion of patria. Patrimony and therefore patria are thus intimately linked with the idea of "generating"; but the word "nation" is also etymologically linked with birth (cf. the Latin word *natus* meaning "born").

The term "nation" designates a community based in a given territory and distinguished from other nations by its culture. Catholic social doctrine holds that the family and the nation are both natural societies, not the product of mere convention. Therefore, in human history they cannot be replaced by anything else. For example, the nation cannot be replaced by the State, even though the nation tends naturally to establish itself as a State, as we see from the history of individual European nations including Poland. In his work *Wyzwolenie* (Liberation), Stanisław Wyspiański wrote: "The nation must exist as a State . . ."[16] Still less is it possible to identify the nation with so-called democratic society, since here it is a case of two distinct, albeit interconnected orders. Democratic society is closer to the State than is the nation. Yet the nation is the ground on which the State is born. The issue of democracy comes later, in the arena of internal politics.

After these preliminary remarks about the nation, it is good to turn once again to Sacred Scripture: here we find the elements of an authentic theology of the nation. This is especially true for Israel. The Old Testament describes the genealogy of this nation, chosen by the Lord as his own people. The term "genealogy" usually refers to biological ancestors. Yet we can also speak of genealogy, perhaps even more validly, in a spiritual sense. Our thoughts turn here to Abraham. Not only do the Israelites trace their ancestry to him, but in a spiritual sense, so too do Christians (cf. Rom 4:11–12) and Muslims. The story of Abraham and his call by God, of his unusual paternity, of the birth of Isaac — all this illustrates how the road to nationhood passes through "generation" via the family and the clan.

At the beginning, then, there is an act of generation. Abraham's wife, Sarah, already advanced in years, gives birth to a son. Abraham now has a descendant in the flesh, and gradually from his family a clan is formed. The Book of Genesis recounts the successive stages in the development of this clan: from Abraham, through Isaac, down to Jacob. The patriarch Jacob has twelve sons, and those twelve sons, in their turn, beget the twelve tribes which constitute the nation of Israel.

God chose that nation, confirming their election through his mighty acts in history, beginning with their deliverance from Egypt under the leadership of Moses. From the time of the great law-giver onward, we can speak of an Israelite nation, even if at first it consisted purely of families and clans. Yet the history of Israel cannot be reduced to this alone. It also has a spiritual dimension. God chose this nation in order to reveal himself, in and through Israel, to the world. This revelation has its starting point in Abraham and reaches its culmination in the mission of Moses. God speaks to Moses "face to face," and through him he guides the spiritual life of Israel. It was their faith in the one God, Creator of heaven and earth, which defined the spiritual life of Israel — and alongside their faith, the Decalogue, that is, the moral law inscribed on the tablets of stone received by Moses on Mount Sinai.

Israel's mission is defined as "Messianic" because from that nation the Messiah was to come, the Anointed one of the Lord. "When the time had fully come, God sent forth his son" (Gal 4:4), who became man through the action of the Holy Spirit in the womb of a daughter of Israel, Mary of Nazareth. The mystery of the Incarnation, foundational for the Church, forms part of the theology of the nation. In becoming flesh, that is, in becoming man, the consubstantial Son, eternal Word of the Father, initiated a "generation" of a different order. It was generation "from the Holy Spirit." Its fruit is our supernatural sonship, our adoptive sonship. This is not about being born "of the flesh," in the words of the Evangelist Saint John. It is about being "born not of blood nor of the will of the flesh nor of the will of man, but of God" (cf. Jn 1:13). Those who are born "of God" become members of the "divine nation," to use an apt formula dear to Ignacy Różycki. It resembles the expression "People of God," which gained currency through the Second Vatican Council. In using this image in the constitution *Lumen Gentium*, the Council no doubt intends to refer to those who "were generated of God" through the grace of the Redeemer, the incarnate Son of God, who died and rose again for our salvation.

Israel is the only nation whose history is recounted in Sacred Scripture. It is a history which forms part of divine Revelation: here God reveals himself to humanity. In the "fullness of time," after having spoken in many and various ways to men, he himself became man. The mystery of the Incarnation also forms part of the history of Israel, although at the same time it leads into the history of the new Israel, that is the people of the New Covenant. "All men are called to belong to the new People of God . . . The one People of God is accordingly present in all the nations of the earth, since its citizens, who are taken from all nations, are of a kingdom whose nature is not earthly but heavenly."[17] In other words, this means that the history of all nations is called to take its place in the history of salvation. Christ came into the world to bring salvation to all. The Church, the People of God founded on the New Covenant, is the new and universal Israel: here every nation has equal rights of citizenship.

14. History

"The history of all nations is called to enter into the history of salvation." In this statement we discover a new dimension within the concepts of "nation" and "native land": the salvation-history dimension. Holy Father, how would you describe this very important aspect in more detail?

Broadly speaking, it could be said that the whole created universe is subject to time and therefore has a history. Living beings have a particular kind of history. Yet not one of them, no other animal species possesses a historical dimension of the kind that we attribute to man, or to nations, or to the entire human family. Man's historicity is expressed in his specific capacity to objectify history. He is not simply subject to the course of events, nor does he limit himself to acting and behaving in a certain way as an individual or as a member of a group: he also has the capacity to reflect on his history and to objectify it, giving an account of the way it unfolds stage by stage. Individual human families have a similar capacity, as do human societies, and especially nations.

Like individuals, then, nations are endowed with historical memory. So it is understandable that they should seek to record in writing what they remember. In this way, history becomes historiography. People write the history of the particular group to which they belong. Sometimes they also write their personal history, but more important for our purposes is what they write about their respective nations. And the histories of nations, objectified and recorded in writing, are among the essential elements of culture — the element which determines the nation's identity in the temporal dimension. "Can history ever swim against the tide of conscience?" I asked this question years ago in a poem entitled "Thinking my country."[18] It arises from reflection on the concepts of nation and patriotism. In the poem I tried to formulate a response. Perhaps it is worth quoting some extracts from the poem here:

Freedom — a continuing conquest,
It cannot simply be possessed!
It comes as a gift, but keeping it is
   a struggle.

Gift and struggle are inscribed on
   pages, hidden yet open.
For freedom you pay with all your
   being, therefore call that your
   freedom
which allows you, in paying the
   price,
to possess yourself ever anew.
At such a price do we enter history
   and touch her epochs.
Where is the dividing line between
   those generations who paid too
   little
and those who paid too much?
On which side of that line are we?

. . .

Over the struggles of conscience,
   history places a layer of events,
Brimming with victories and
   defeats.
History does not conceal them — it
   proclaims them.

. . .

How weak the people that accepts
   defeat,
that forgets its call to keep vigil

until its hour should come.
The hours continually return on
　　the great clockface of history.
Herein the liturgy of life.
That vigil is the Lord's word and
　　the people's word
which comes to us ever anew.
The hours become a psalm of
　　ceaseless conversions.
Let us take part in the Eucharist of
　　the worlds.

The text ends thus:

O earth, you do not cease
to be an atom of our age.
Learning new hope,
we pass through this time toward a
　　new earth.
And we raise you, ancient earth,
fruit of the love of generations,
the love that overcame hate.[19]

The history of every individual, and
therefore of every people, possesses a markedly eschatological dimension. The Second
Vatican Council has much to say on this
subject throughout its teaching, and especially in the constitutions *Lumen Gentium*
and *Gaudium et Spes*. It is an important

way of reading history in the light of the Gospel. The eschatological aspect means that human life makes sense and the history of nations also makes sense. Admittedly, it is people and not nations that have to face God's judgment, but in the judgment pronounced on individuals, nations too are in some way judged.

Can there be such a thing as an eschatology of the nation? Nations have an exclusively historical meaning, whereas man's vocation is eschatological. Yet man's vocation leaves its mark on the history of nations. This is another idea that I wanted to express in the poem quoted above, perhaps a further echo of the Second Vatican Council's teaching.

Peoples recount their history through narratives recorded in documents of many different types, through which national culture takes shape. The principal instrument of this process is language, with which man expresses the truth about the world and about himself, and he shares with others the fruits of his investigations in various fields of knowledge. In this way, communication takes place, leading to greater knowledge of the truth and thereby deepening and consolidating the identities of the respective interlocutors.

In the light of these considerations we can now clarify further the concept of "native land." In my address to UNESCO, I recalled the experience of my own native land, and this struck a particular chord with delegates from societies whose native lands and national identities were still in the process of formation. We Poles passed through that phase around the turn of the tenth and eleventh centuries, as we were reminded on the occasion of the millennium of Poland's baptism. When we speak of Poland's baptism, we are not simply referring to the sacrament of Christian initiation received by the first historical sovereign of Poland, but also to the event which was decisive for the birth of the nation and the formation of its Christian identity. In this sense, the date of Poland's baptism marks a turning point. Poland as a nation emerges from its prehistory at that moment and begins to exist in history. Prehistory records the presence of individual Slav tribes.

In ethnic terms, perhaps the most significant event for the foundation of the nation was the union of two great tribes: the Polanians of the North and the Vistulans of the South. Yet these were not the only tribes. The Polish nation also incorporated the Silesian, Pomeranian, and

Mazovian peoples. From the time of Poland's baptism, the different tribes began to exist as the Polish nation.

15. Nation and Culture

Holy Father, in discussing the cultural and historical identity of the nation, you are addressing a complex subject. Certain questions present themselves: How is culture to be understood? What does it mean and what is its genesis? How do we define more precisely the role of culture in the life of a nation?

The origins of history — as every believer knows — are found in the Book of Genesis. Likewise the origins of culture are traceable to that same source. Everything is contained in these simple words: "The Lord God formed man of dust from the ground and breathed into his nostrils the breath of life, and man became a living being" (Gn 2:7). This decision by the Creator was unlike any other. Whereas in creating other beings God simply says: "Let there be . . . ," in this one case he, as it were, goes back into himself for a kind of Trinitarian consultation and then decides: "Let us make man in our image, according to our likeness" (Gn

1:26). The Biblical author goes on to say: "God created man in his image; in the image of God he created him; male and female he created them. God blessed them and said to them: Be fruitful and multiply, fill the earth and subdue it" (Gn 1:27–28). Finally, on the sixth day of creation: "God saw everything that he had made, and indeed, it was very good" (Gn 1:31). We find these words in the first chapter of the Book of Genesis, commonly attributed to the so-called "priestly tradition."

In the second chapter, the work of the Yahwist redactor, the theme of man's creation is treated more extensively, more descriptively, and more psychologically. It begins with man's awareness of his solitude, on being summoned into existence in the midst of the visible universe. He gives suitable names to the creatures surrounding him. And having considered all living beings in turn, he realizes that not one of them is like him. He feels alone in the world. God provides for him in his loneliness by deciding to create woman. According to the Biblical text, the Creator causes a deep sleep to fall upon the man, during which he forms Eve from one of his ribs. As he awakes from sleep, the man looks with amazement upon the new creature like himself and he cries out with joy: "This at last is bone of my bones and flesh of my flesh" (Gn 2:23). In this way, the female of the human species is placed in the world alongside the male. There follows the famous passage which reveals the profound commitment involved in living as a couple: "Therefore a man leaves his father and his mother and cleaves to his wife, and they become one flesh" (Gn 2:24). This union in the flesh leads to the mysterious experience of parenthood.

The Book of Genesis goes on to recount that the two human beings, created by God as male and female, were both naked and felt no shame. They remained thus until the moment when they allowed themselves to be seduced by the serpent, symbol of the evil spirit. It was the serpent who persuaded them to take the fruit of the tree of knowledge of good and evil, encouraging them with these insinuating words to disobey God's clear command: "You will not die! For God knows that when you eat of it your eyes will be opened and you will be like God, knowing good and evil" (Gn 3:4–5). When both the man and the woman acted on the promptings of the evil spirit, they knew they were naked and they began to feel shame at their own bodies. They had lost their original innocence. The third chapter of the Book of Genesis outlines most eloquently the consequences of original sin for both the woman and the man, and for their mutual relationship. Yet God speaks of a woman in the future whose offspring will crush the serpent's head, that is to say he foretells the coming of the Redeemer and his work of salvation (cf. Gn 3:15).

Keeping in mind this brief sketch of man's original state, we will now return to the first chapter of the Book of Genesis, where we read that God created man in his image and likeness and said: "Be fruitful and multiply, and fill the earth and subdue it; and have dominion over the fish of the sea" (Gn 1:28). These words are the earliest and most complete definition of human culture. To subdue and have dominion over the earth means to discover and confirm the truth about being human, about the humanity that belongs equally to man and to woman. To us and to our humanity, God has entrusted the visible world as a gift and also as a task. In other words, he has assigned us a particular mission: to accomplish the truth about ourselves and about the world. We must be guided by the truth about ourselves, so as to be able to structure the visible world according to truth, correctly using it to serve our purposes, without abusing it. In other words, this two-fold truth about the world and about ourselves provides the basis for every intervention by us upon creation.

This mission to the visible world, as outlined in the Book of Genesis, has evolved throughout history, gaining pace to a remarkable degree in modern times. It all began with the invention of machines: since that time we have transformed not only the raw materials supplied by nature but also our own products. In this sense human work has acquired the character of industrial production. Yet the essential norm governing industrial production never changes: we have to remain faithful to the truth about ourselves and about the object of our work, whether we are handling natural raw materials or man-made products.

In the opening pages of the Book of Genesis, we discover the essence of culture, and we grasp its original and fundamental meaning; from here we can proceed, step by step, toward the truth of modern industrial civilization. From the beginning until now, civilization has always been linked to the growth of our knowledge of the truth about the world, that is to say the growth of science. This is its cognitive dimension. We could usefully take time to analyze in depth the first three chapters of the Book of Genesis, from which all this is ultimately derived. Of course human culture depends not only on our knowledge of the outside world, but also on our knowledge of ourselves, including our twofold gender: "male and female he created them" (Gn 1:27). The first chapter of the Book of Genesis completes this illustration of culture when it relates God's command concerning human generation: "Be fruitful and multiply, fill the earth and subdue it" (Gn 1:28). The second and third chapters provide further material that helps us to understand God's plan. Here we read about man's solitude, about the creation of a being like him, about the wonder felt by the man on seeing the woman drawn from his flesh, about the vocation to marriage, and, finally, about the entire history of original innocence, tragically lost through original sin — all this expresses the importance for culture of a love based on knowledge. This love is the source of new life. More fundamentally still, it is the source of a creative wonder that seeks expression through art.

Deeply ingrained in human culture, from the outset, is the element of beauty. The beauty of the universe is, as it were, reflected in the eyes of God, of whom it is said: "God saw everything that he had made, and indeed, it was very good" (Gn 1:31). The predicate "very good" is applied especially to the first man and woman, created in God's image and likeness, in all their original innocence and in the nakedness characteristic of the time preceding the Fall. This is what lies at the very heart of the culture that is expressed in works of art, whether they be paintings, sculptures, buildings, pieces of music, or other products of creative imagination and thought.

Every nation draws life from the works of its own culture. We Poles, for example, trace ours back to the song *Bogurodzica* (*Mother of God*), the earliest Polish poetry to be written down, and also to the centuries-old melody which accompanies it: from this and all that followed, we draw life. When I was in Gniezno in 1979, during my first pilgrimage to Poland, I spoke of this to the young people gathered on Lech's Hill. The song *Bogurodzica* comes specifically from the Gniezno tradition in Polish culture. This is the tradition of Adalbert, Poland's patron saint, to whom the song is actually attributed. It is a tradition stretching back through centuries. The song *Bogurodzica* became the national anthem, and it guided the Polish and Lithuanian armies in their battle against the Teutonic Order at Grunwald.[20] There is a distinct tradition, originating from Kraków and linked to the cult of Saint Stanislaus. It found expression in the Latin hymn, *Gaude, Mater Polonia*, still sung in Latin today, just as *Bogurodzica* is sung in old Polish. These two traditions intertwine. Indeed, for a long time Latin, alongside Polish, was the language of Polish culture. Much poetry was written in Latin, including that of Janicius, for example, as well as political and moral treatises, like those of Andrzej Frycz Modrzewski or Orzechowski, and likewise the work of Nicolaus Copernicus: *De revolutionibus orbium caelestium*. Literature in Polish underwent a parallel development, from Mikołaj Rey to Jan Kochanowski, with whom it attained renown throughout Europe. Kochanowski's *Psalter of David* (*Psałterz Dawidów*) is still sung today. His *Laments* (*Treny*) on the death of his daughter mark a high point in lyric poetry. Moreover, *The Farewell of the Greek Envoys* (*Odprawa posłów greckich*) is a magnificent play drawing upon ancient models.

What I have said here reminds me of my address to UNESCO on the role of culture in the life of nations. The impact of that speech lay in the fact that it offered not a theory of culture but a testimony to culture — the simple testimony of one who, through personal experience, could express what culture had meant in the history of his own nation and what it represents in the history of every nation. What is the role of culture in the life of young African nations, for example? We must ask how this common treasury of the human race, the treasury of so many different cultures, can be built up over time, and we must ask how best to respect the proper relationship between economics and culture without destroying this greater human good for the sake of profit, in deference to the overwhelming power of one-sided market forces. It matters little, in fact, whether this kind of tyranny is imposed by Marxist totalitarianism or by Western liberalism. In the course of my address I said, among other things:

> Man lives a really human life thanks to culture . . . Culture is a specific way of man's 'existing' and 'being' . . . Culture is that through which man, as man, becomes more man, 'is' more . . . The nation is, in fact, the great community of men who are united by various ties,

but above all, precisely by culture. The nation exists 'through' culture and 'for' culture and it is therefore the great educator of men in order that they may 'be more' in the community. It is this community which possesses a history that goes beyond the history of the individual and the family . . . I am the son of a nation which has lived the greatest experiences of history, which its neighbors have condemned to death several times, but which has survived and remained itself. It has kept its identity, and it has kept, in spite of partitions and foreign occupations, its national sovereignty, not by relying on the resources of physical power but solely by relying on its culture. This culture turned out, under the circumstances, to be more powerful than all other forces. What I say here concerning the right of the nation to the foundation of its culture and its future is not, therefore, the echo of any 'nationalism', but it is always a question of a stable element of human experience and of the humanistic perspective of man's development. There exists a fundamental sovereignty of society, which is manifested in the culture of the nation. It is a question of the sovereignty through which, at the same time, man is supremely sovereign.[21]

What I said on that occasion about the role of culture in national life was my personal testimony to the Polish spirit. My convictions on this subject had already acquired a universal dimension. At that time, on June 2, 1980, I was in the second year of my pontificate. I had completed a few of my apostolic journeys: in Latin America, in Africa, and in Asia. During those journeys I became convinced that the experience I had gained of the history of my native land, and the knowledge I had acquired of the value of the "nation," created a bond between me and the people I was meeting. Indeed, the experience of my own native land helped me greatly in my encounters with people and nations all over the world.

My words to UNESCO about national identity as expressed through culture were particularly well received by the delegates from Third World countries. Some delegates from Western Europe — so it seemed to me — had greater reservations. One might ask why. One of my first apostolic journeys was to Zaire, in Equatorial Africa: an enormous country, in which 250 languages are spoken, including four principal languages, and with a population made up of many different clans and tribes. How can a single nation be formed out of such great diversity? Almost all African countries are in a similar situation. Maybe in terms of the development of their national consciousness they have reached a stage corresponding to the era of Mieszko I or Boleslaw the Brave in Polish history. Our first kings faced similar challenges. The thesis which I presented at UNESCO about the formation of national identity through culture struck a chord with the most vital needs of all young nations in search of ways of consolidating their own sovereignty.

Modern Western European countries have arrived at a stage which could be defined as "post-identity." It seems to me that one of the effects of the Second World War was to form a common mentality among European citizens, against the background of a continent tending toward unification. Obviously, there are many reasons for this trend toward a united Europe. One reason is surely the gradual demise of exclusively nationalistic categories in people's sense of identity. Western European nations, as a rule, do not consider that they risk losing their national identity. The French are not afraid of ceasing to be French by virtue of their entry into the European Union, and the same is true of the Italians, the Spanish, etc. Nor are the Poles afraid of this, although the history of their national identity is much more complex.

Historically, the Polish spirit has had a very interesting evolution. Probably no other European nation has evolved in quite the same way. From the outset, at the time when the Polanian, Vistulan, and other tribes were merging, it was the Polish spirit of the Piast dynasty that provided the unifying element: theirs was, so to speak, the "pure" Polish spirit. Later, for five centuries, the Polish spirit of the Jagiellonian era prevailed.[22] This made possible the emergence of a Republic embracing many nations, many cultures, many religions. All Poles bear within themselves a sense of this religious and national diversity. I myself come from Małopolska, from the territory of the ancient Vistulan tribe, closely linked to Kraków. And yet in Małopolska — and perhaps more in Kraków than elsewhere — there was a sense of proximity to Vilnius, to Lviv, and to the East.

A further element of great importance in the ethnic composition of Poland was the presence of the Jews. I remember that at least a third of my classmates at elementary school in Wadowice were Jews. At secondary school they were fewer. With some I was on very friendly terms. And what struck me about some of them was their Polish patriotism. Fundamental to the Polish spirit, then, is multiplicity and pluralism, not limitation and closure. It seems, though, that the "Jagiellonian" dimension of the Polish spirit, mentioned above, has sadly ceased to be an evident feature of our time.

THINKING "EUROPE"
(POLAND — EUROPE — CHURCH)

16. Europe as "Native Land"

After reflecting on the basic concepts of native land, nation, freedom, and culture, it seems appropriate, Holy Father, to return to the theme of Europe, to look at its relationship with the Church and to consider the role of Poland within this broader context. Holy Father, what is your vision of Europe? How do you assess the events of the past, the present situation of the Continent, and its prospects in the third millennium? What are Europe's responsibilities for the future of mankind?

A Pole cannot reflect in depth on his native land without speaking of Europe and discussing the way the Church has helped to shape these two realities. They are clearly distinct from one another, yet their mutual influence is profound. Inevitably, therefore, our discussion will touch upon one or other of these elements: native land, Europe, the Church, the world.

Poland is part of Europe. It is a clearly defined territory located in the European Continent, and it came into contact with Latin Christianity through neighboring Bohemia. When we speak of the birth of Christianity in Poland, we should cast our minds back to the origins of Christianity in Europe. In the Acts of the Apostles, we read that Saint Paul, while proclaiming the Gospel in Asia Minor, received a mysterious call to cross the border between the two continents (cf. Acts 16:9). The evangelization of Europe began at that moment. The Apostles themselves, especially Paul and Peter, brought the Gospel to Greece and Rome; with the passing of centuries, the seeds sown by the Apostles yielded abundant fruit. The Gospel entered Europe by a variety of routes: the Italian peninsula, the area that is now France and Germany, the Iberian peninsula, the British Isles, and Scandinavia. It is significant that one of the main centers from which missionaries set out, other than Rome, should have been Ireland. In the East, Byzantine Christianity spread outward from Constantinople, likewise the later Slav form. Of particular importance for the Slav world was the mission of the brothers Cyril and Methodius, who set off on their task of evangelization from Constantinople, while remaining in contact with Rome. At that time, of course, there was no division between Christians of the East and those of the West.

Why do we begin our discussion of Europe by speaking of evangelization? Perhaps the simplest answer is that it was evangelization which formed Europe, giving birth to the civilization of its peoples and their cultures. As the faith spread through the Continent, it favored the formation of individual European peoples, sowing the seeds of cultures different in character, but linked together by a patrimony of common values derived from the Gospel. In this way the pluralism of national cultures developed upon a platform of values shared throughout the Continent. That is how it was in the first millennium, and also to some degree, despite the emergence of divisions, in the second millennium: Europe continued to live by the unity of its founding values, amid the pluralism of national cultures.

In arguing that evangelization made a fundamental contribution to the formation of Europe, we do not intend to devalue the influence of the ancient world. The Church herself, in carrying out her task of evangelization, absorbed and transformed the older cultural patrimony. I am speaking principally of the heritage of Greece and Rome, but I also include that of the peoples the Church encountered as she spread throughout the Continent. In the evangelization of Europe, which supplied a certain cultural unity to the Latin world in the West and the Byzantine world in the East, the Church acted according to the criteria of what we now call inculturation. She contributed to the growth of native and national cultures. How fitting, therefore, that the Church should have proclaimed first Saint Benedict and then Saints Cyril and Methodius patrons of Europe, thereby pointing to the great work of inculturation that took place over the centuries, and reminding us that the Church in Europe must breathe with "two lungs." This is a metaphor, of course, but an eloquent one. Just as a healthy organism needs two lungs in order to breathe properly, so too the Church, as a spiritual organism, needs these two traditions in order to attain more fully to the riches of Revelation.

The long formation of Christian Europe continued throughout the first millennium and much of the second. In the process, not only did the Christian character of Europe take shape but also the European spirit. The fruits of this process are perhaps more visible today than they were in patristic or medieval times. In those days, of course, much of the world was unknown. To the East of Europe lay the mysterious Asian Continent with its ancient cultures and religions older than Christianity. The enormous American Continent was totally unknown until the end of the fifteenth century. The same obviously applies to Australia, which was discovered even later. As for Africa, in ancient and medieval times only the northern, Mediterranean part was known. Therefore mature reflection in "European" categories could take place only later, when the entire globe began to be explored. In earlier times, we thought in categories associated with particular empires: firstly the Egyptian Empire, then the constantly changing empires of the Middle East, then the Empire of Alexander the Great, and, finally, the Roman Empire.

The Acts of the Apostles recount an event of great significance for the evangelization of Europe and for the history of the European spirit. I refer to what happened at the Areopagus in Athens, when Saint Paul arrived there and delivered a deservedly famous speech:

Athenians, I see how extremely religious you are in every way. For as I went through the city and looked carefully at the objects of your worship, I found among them an altar with the inscription, 'To an unknown God'. What therefore you worship as unknown, this I proclaim to you. The God who made the world and everything in it, he who is Lord of heaven and earth, does not live in shrines made by human hands, nor is he served by human hands, as though he needed anything, since he himself gives to all mortals life and breath and all things. From one ancestor he made all nations to inhabit the whole earth, and he allotted the times of their existence and the boundaries of the places where they would live, so that they would search for God in the hope that they might feel after him and find him — though indeed he is not far from each one of us. For 'In him we live and move and have our being'; as even some of your own poets have said, 'For we are indeed his offspring.' Since we are God's offspring, we ought not to think that the deity is like gold, or silver, or stone, an image formed by the art and imagination of mortals. While God has overlooked the times of human ignorance, now he commands all people everywhere to repent, because he has fixed a day on which he will have the world judged in righteousness by a man whom he has appointed, and of this he has given assurance to all by raising him from the dead. (Acts 17:22–31)

As we read this passage, we observe that Paul arrived at the Areopagus well prepared: he knew Greek philosophy and poetry. In his address to the Athenians he started out from the idea of the "unknown God," to whom they had dedicated an altar. He described the eternal attributes of this God: pure spirit, wisdom, omnipotence, omnipresence, and justice. In this way, through a kind of theodicy in which he appealed solely to rational data, Paul prepared his hearers to listen to the proclamation of the mystery of the Incarnation. He went on to speak of the Revelation of God in Man, in Christ crucified and risen. But it was at this point that his Athenian audience, hitherto seemingly well disposed to what he had been saying, began to react negatively. "When they heard of the resurrection of the dead, some mocked; but others said 'We will hear you again about this' " (Acts

17:32). So it was that Paul's mission at the Areopagus ended in failure, even if some of his listeners remained with him and believed. Among these, according to tradition, was Dionysius the Areopagite.

Why have I quoted here the whole of Paul's address at the Areopagus? Because it serves as an introduction to what Christianity would achieve in Europe. After the magnificent progress of evangelization, which in the course of the first millennium spread to virtually every European country, came the Christian universalism of the Middle Ages: the era of simple, strong, and profound faith; the era of Romanesque and Gothic Cathedrals and stupendous *Summae theologiae*. Europe's evangelization seemed not only complete, but thoroughly mature, not just in terms of philosophical and theological thought, but also in sacred art and architecture, in social solidarity (guilds, confraternities, hospitals, . . .). Yet from 1054 onward, this seemingly mature Europe was torn apart by the profound wound of the "Eastern schism." Within the single organism of the Church, the two lungs had ceased to function together: each had begun to form an almost independent organism. This division cast a shadow over the spiritual life of Christian

Europe from the beginning of the second millennium.

The arrival of modern times brought further disputes and divisions, this time in the West. Martin Luther's stand marked the onset of the Protestant Reformation. He was followed by others, such as Calvin and Zwingli. The rift between the Church in the British Isles and the See of Peter should be seen in a similar light. Having been united throughout the Middle Ages from the religious perspective, Western Europe suffered grave divisions on the threshold of modern times, and these became more deeply entrenched in the centuries that followed. There were political consequences, according to the principle *cuius regio eius religio* — the religion of a territory is to be determined by the ruler. Tragically, these consequences included wars of religion.

All this forms part of European history and it has weighed heavily on the European spirit, shaping its vision of the future and anticipating further divisions and new sufferings that would emerge later. Yet it should be pointed out that faith in Christ, crucified and risen, remained a common denominator for Christians of the Reformation era. They were divided in their relationship with the Church and with

Rome, but they did not reject the truth of Christ's Resurrection, as some of Saint Paul's listeners had done at the Areopagus in Athens. Or at least, not initially. Later, unfortunately, it would gradually come to that.

The rejection of Christ and, in particular, of his Paschal Mystery — the Cross and Resurrection — entered European thought in the late seventeenth and early eighteenth centuries, the era of the Enlightenment. First came the French Enlightenment, followed by the English and German versions. In all its different forms, the Enlightenment was opposed to what Europe had become as a result of evangelization. Its exponents were rather like Paul's listeners at the Areopagus. Most of them did not reject the existence of the "unknown God" as a spiritual and transcendent Being in whom "we live and move and have our being" (Acts 17:28). Yet the most radical Enlightenment thinkers, more than fifteen centuries after Paul's address at the Areopagus, did reject the truth about Christ, the Son of God who had revealed himself by becoming man, being born of the Virgin at Bethlehem, proclaiming the Good News, and eventually giving his life for the sins of all mankind. So-called "Enlightened" European thought tried to dissociate itself from this God-Man, who died and rose again, and every effort was made to exclude him from the history of the Continent. This approach still has many stubbornly faithful adherents among thinkers and politicians of today.

The exponents of postmodern thought are critical of both the positive heritage and the errors of the Enlightenment. At times, however, their criticism is excessive, because they even reject Enlightenment positions on humanism, confidence in reason, progress. Yet the polemical attitude of many Enlightenment thinkers toward Christianity is undeniable. The real "cultural drama" still unfolding today consists of a supposed tension between Christianity and ideas like those just mentioned, although in actual fact these ideas are profoundly rooted in the Christian tradition.

Before continuing with this analysis of the European spirit, I should like to refer to another New Testament text: the passage where Jesus presents the allegory of the vine and the branches. Christ says: "I am the vine, you are the branches" (Jn 15:5). Then he develops this great metaphor, sketching as it were a theology of Incarnation and Redemption. He is the vine, the Father is the vine grower, and individual Christians are the branches. Jesus proposed this image to the Apostles on the eve of his Passion: man as a branch of the vine. Blaise Pascal comes close to this idea when he describes man as a "thinking reed."[23] Yet the most profound and essential aspect of the metaphor is what Christ says regarding the cultivation of the vine. God, man's Creator, cares for his creature. As the vine grower, he cultivates it. He does so in his own particular way. He grafts mankind onto the stock of the divinity of his only-begotten Son. The Son who is eternal and consubstantial with the Father becomes man for this very reason.

Why this "cultivation" on God's part? Is it possible to graft a human branch onto the Vine that is God incarnate? The answer given by Revelation is clear: from the beginning, man is called into existence in the image and likeness of God (cf. Gn 1:27), and so, from the beginning, his humanity already conceals within itself something of the divine. His humanity, then, can be "cultivated" in this extraordinary way. Moreover, in God's plan of salvation, it is only by agreeing to be grafted onto Christ's divine Vine that man can become fully himself. Were he to refuse this grafting, he would effectively condemn himself to an incomplete humanity.

Why, at this point in our reflections on Europe, do I speak of Christ's parable of the vine and the branches? Perhaps because it offers us the best explanation of the drama of the European Enlightenment. In rejecting Christ, or at least in marginalizing his place in human history and culture, this development in European thought signaled a revolution. Man was cut off from the "vine," he was no longer grafted onto that Vine which guarantees him the possibility of attaining to the fullness of his humanity. It could be said that, in a qualitatively new and previously unknown way, at least on such a scale, a path had been opened up that would lead toward the devastating experiences of evil which were to follow.

According to Saint Thomas's definition, evil is the absence of a good that ought to be present in a given being. A good which ought to be present in man, as a being created in the image and likeness of God and redeemed by Christ from sin, is that of participation in the nature and the life of God himself, since Christ won this extraordinary privilege for us through the mystery of the Incarnation and Redemption. To deprive man of such a good is equivalent, in the language of the Gospel, to cutting the "branch" off from the vine. Consequently, the human branch cannot develop toward that fullness which the "vine grower," that is, the Creator, intended and planned for it.

17. The Evangelization of Central and Eastern Europe

The evangelization of Central and Eastern parts of Europe, as Your Holiness has mentioned, followed a path of its own. This surely had an influence on the cultural characteristics of those peoples.

It is right to give separate treatment to the evangelization which originated in Byzantium, aptly symbolized by Saints Cyril and Methodius, the Apostles of the Slavs. They were Greeks, originally from Thessalonica. They undertook the evangelization of the Slavs, setting out from the territory of present-day Bulgaria. Their first concern was to learn the local language, assigning its sounds to a certain number of graphic symbols which formed the first Slav alphabet, known thereafter as "Cyrillic." This, with a few changes, is still in use today in Eastern Slav countries, while Western Slavs have adopted the Latin alphabet, using Latin initially as the language of the cultivated classes, then gradually building up their own literature.

Cyril and Methodius were sent on their mission by the Duke of Great Moravia, into territory which belonged to that State in the ninth century. They probably also reached the land of the Vistulan tribe, beyond the Carpathians. They certainly went as far as Pannonia, that is to say present-day Hungary, and also to Croatia, Bosnia and Herzegovina, and the area around Ochrida, the region of Slav Macedonia. They left disciples who continued their missionary activity. The two saintly brothers also influenced the evangelization of the Slavs in the territories to the north of the Black Sea. In fact, through the baptism of Saint Vladimir in 988, the evangelization of the Slavs extended throughout Kievan Rus, and later spread gradually into the north of present-day Russia, as far as the Urals. In the thirteenth century, after the Mongol invasion which destroyed Kievan Rus, this evangelization went through a severe trial of historic proportions. Yet the new religious and political centers in the north, especially in Moscow, not only succeeded in protecting the Christian tradition in its Slavo-Byzantine form, but also in spreading it within Europe as far as the Urals and beyond, into the territory of Siberia and Northern Asia.

All this forms part of European history and reflects, in some way, the nature of the European spirit. If, under the influence of the principle *cuius regio eius religio,* the post-Reformation period led to wars of religion, many Christians recognized that these wars were contrary to the spirit of the Gospel. Gradually they succeeded in establishing the principle of religious liberty, which would allow people to choose religious denomination and ecclesial membership for themselves. With the passage of time, moreover, the various Christian denominations, especially those of an evangelical Protestant bent, began to seek understandings and agreements: the initial steps of what was to grow into the ecumenical movement. As far as the Catholic Church is concerned, a decisive moment in this process was the Second Vatican Council, in which she definitively expressed her own position regarding all the Churches and ecclesial communities outside Catholic unity, committing herself wholeheartedly to the ecumenical endeavor. This was of great importance for the future full unity of all Christians. In the twentieth century more than ever before, Christ's followers realized that they could not do other than seek after the unity for which Jesus prayed on the eve of his Passion: "That they may all be one. As you, Father, are in me and I am in you, may they also be in us, so that the world may believe that you have sent me" (Jn 17:21). Given that the Patriarchates of the Orthodox East are also actively engaging in ecumenical dialogue, we may cherish the hope of full unity in a not-too-distant future. The apostolic see, for its part, is determined to do whatever it can to promote this end through dialogue both with Orthodoxy and with individual Churches and ecclesial communities in the West.

As we read in the Acts of the Apostles, Christianity came to Europe from Jerusalem via Asia Minor. It was from Jerusalem that the missionary roads leading Christ's Apostles "to the ends of the earth" (Acts 1:8) originally set out. Yet, from apostolic times, the center of missionary outreach shifted to Europe, firstly to Rome, where the holy Apostles Peter and Paul bore witness to Christ, then to Constantinople, that is to say, Byzantium. So evangelization had its two principal centers in Rome and in Byzantium. From these cities the missionaries set out in fulfilment of Christ's command: "Go therefore and make disciples of all nations, baptizing them in the name of the

Father and of the Son and of the Holy Spirit" (Mt 28:19). The effects of this missionary activity are still evident in modern Europe. They are reflected in the cultural orientation of its peoples. If the missionaries from Rome initiated a process of inculturation that gave rise to Latin Christianity, those from Byzantium promoted its Byzantine form: first Greek and later Slav, "Cyrillo-Methodian." These were the two principal paths along which the evangelization of the Continent proceeded.

Gradually, with the passage of the centuries, evangelization reached beyond the boundaries of Europe. The epic story is a glorious one, though the issue of colonialism has cast a shadow over it. In the modern sense of this term, colonialism began with the discovery of America. The American continent itself was the first great European "colony": in its southern and central part through the activity of the Spanish and the Portuguese, and in the northern part through the initiative of the French and the English. Colonialism was a passing phenomenon. A few centuries after the discovery of America, both the south and the north of the continent saw new societies emerging and new post-colonial states, which to an ever greater degree have become true partners with Europe.

The celebration of the five-hundredth anniversary of the discovery of America provided an opportunity to study the important question of the relationship between the growth of American society in both north and south and the rights of indigenous peoples. This fundamental question arises whenever colonization occurs. It also applies to Africa. It comes from the fact that colonization always implies importing and grafting "the new" onto an older stem. Up to a point, it assists the progress of indigenous peoples, but it also brings with it a form of expropriation not only of their land but also of their spiritual patrimony. How did this problem manifest itself in North and South America? What moral evaluation should we give to it in the light of the different historical situations that have emerged? It is right to ask these questions, and we have an obligation to seek a satisfactory response. Similarly we have an obligation to acknowledge the mistakes made by the colonial settlers, and as far as possible, to make efforts to provide for their reparation.

In any case, the issue of colonialism belongs to the history of Europe and of the European spirit. Europe is a small but highly developed continent. Providence, one might say, has entrusted to Europe the task of initiating a wide-ranging exchange of goods between various parts of the world, between countries, nations, and peoples. Nor must we forget that the Church's missionary activity all over the world set out from Europe. Having received the Good News of salvation from Jerusalem, Europe — both east and west — became a great center of evangelization for the rest of the world, and, despite all the crises, it has remained so to the present day. Perhaps the situation is changing. Maybe sooner or later the Church in Europe will find that it needs the help of the Church in other continents. Should this happen, it could be interpreted as a kind of settlement of "debts" incurred by those continents toward Europe for the proclamation of the Gospel.

We cannot speak of modern European history without considering the two great revolutions: the French Revolution in the late eighteenth century and the Russian Revolution in the early twentieth century. Both were a reaction against feudalism, which in France took the form of "Enlightened absolutism" and in Russia that of Tsarist "autocracy" (*samodierżawie*). The French Revolution, which claimed many innocent victims, eventually brought Napoleon to power; he proclaimed himself Emperor of the French and succeeded in dominating Europe through his military genius during the first decade of the nineteenth century. After Napoleon's fall, the Congress of Vienna restored the system of Enlightened absolutism to Europe, particularly to those countries responsible for the partition of Poland. The end of the nineteenth century and the beginning of the twentieth reinforced this distribution of power and witnessed the birth and establishment in Europe of younger nations, including Italy.

In the second decade of the twentieth century, the European situation deteriorated, leading to the outbreak of the First World War, a deadly confrontation between the "Great Alliances" — on the one hand France, Britain, and Russia, joined by Italy; on the other hand Germany and Austria. Yet this same conflict enabled some peoples to gain their freedom. When the War ended in 1918, the map of Europe once again included certain States which had hitherto been denied their freedom by powerful invaders. The year 1918 marks the recovery of independence by Poland, Lithuania, Latvia, and Estonia. Farther south, the free

Czechoslovak Republic was born, while some other Central European nations became part of the Yugoslav Federation. Ukraine and Belarus did not achieve their independence at this stage, despite the hopes and aspirations of their peoples. This distribution of power in Europe, representing a new political situation, was to remain in place for barely twenty years.

18. The Positive Fruits of the Enlightenment

The eruption of evil during the First World War had an even more terrifying sequel in the Second and in the crimes of which we spoke earlier. Holy Father, you said that in considering modern Europe we should not limit ourselves to the evil, to the destructive aftermath of the Enlightenment and the French Revolution. That would be too one-sided. How, then, are we to widen our field of vision so as to include also the positive aspects of modern European history?

The European Enlightenment not only led to the carnage of the French Revolution but also bore positive fruits, such as the ideals of liberty, equality, and fraternity, values which are rooted in the Gospel. Even when proclaimed independently, these ideas point naturally to their proper origin. Hence, the French Enlightenment paved the way for a better understanding of human rights. Of course, the Revolution violated those rights in many ways. Yet this was also the time when human rights began to be properly acknowledged and put into effect more forcefully, leaving behind the traditions of feudalism. It should be stressed that these rights were already known to be rooted in the nature of man created by God in his own image, and as such they are proclaimed in Sacred Scripture from the opening pages of the Book of Genesis. Christ himself speaks of them repeatedly; for example, when he says in the Gospel that "the Sabbath was made for man and not man for the Sabbath" (Mk 2:27). With these words, he authoritatively asserts man's higher dignity, definitively indicating the divine foundation of his human rights.

Similarly the rights of nations are linked with the Enlightenment tradition and even with the French Revolution. During this period, that is to say the eighteenth century, the right of nations to exist, to maintain their own culture, and to exercise political sovereignty mattered greatly to many nations on the European continent and elsewhere. It mattered for Poland, which was about to lose its independence despite the constitution of May 3.[24] It mattered particularly, across the ocean, for the United States of America, which was coming into existence at this time. It is significant that these three events — the French Revolution (July 14, 1789), the proclamation of the constitution of May 3 (1791) in Poland, and the Declaration of Independence in the United States of America (July 4, 1776) — took place so close together in time. Yet something similar could be said of several Latin American countries, which were just arriving at a new national consciousness after a long feudal period, and consequently were developing aspirations toward independence from the Spanish or Portuguese crown.

So we see that the demand for liberty, equality, and fraternity was increasing, albeit amid much bloodshed. These ideals shed light upon the history of peoples and nations, at least in Europe and America, thereby ushering in a new historical era. As for the idea of fraternity, which is thoroughly rooted in the Gospel, the period of the French Revolution established it more firmly in the history of Europe and the history of the world. Fraternity is a bond uniting not only men but also nations. The history of the world should be governed by the principle of fraternity among peoples, and not simply by political power games or the imposition of the will of the most powerful, with insufficient regard for the rights of men and nations.

The values of liberty, equality, and fraternity were providential at the beginning of the nineteenth century because this was a period of great social transformation. The capitalism of the early Industrial Revolution did violence to liberty, equality, and fraternity in various ways, allowing the exploitation of man by man in deference to the laws of the market. The Enlightenment vision, especially its concept of freedom, certainly favored the birth of the *Communist Manifesto* by Karl Marx, but it also led, quite independently, to the enunciation of principles of social justice rooted in the Gospel. It is striking how often the logic of Enlightenment thought led to a profound rediscovery of the truths contained in the Gospel. This becomes clear in the great social encyclicals, from *Rerum Novarum* of Leo XIII to *Centesimus Annus* in the late twentieth century.

In the documents of the Second Vatican Council, we find a stimulating synthesis of the relation between Christianity and the Enlightenment. Admittedly the texts do not refer to this directly, but if examined in greater depth in the light of the contemporary cultural context, they offer many valuable insights. The Council's exposition of doctrine adopted a deliberately non-polemical stance. It chose instead to continue the process of inculturation which has accompanied Christianity from the time of the Apostles. Taking their cue from the Council, Christians can engage with the modern world and enter into a constructive dialogue with it. Like the Good Samaritan, they can also come to the aid of suffering man, tending the wounds that he bears at the beginning of this twenty-first century. Care for the needy is incomparably more important than polemics and denunciations concerning, for example, the role of the Enlightenment in paving the way for the great historical catastrophes of the twentieth century. The spirit of the Gospel is seen primarily in this willingness to offer fraternal help to those in need.

"In reality it is only in the mystery of the Word made flesh that the mystery of man truly becomes clear."[25] With these words, the Second Vatican Council expresses the anthropology that lies at the heart of the entire Conciliar Magisterium. Christ not only teaches us the ways of the interior life, but he proposes himself as the "Way" to be followed in order to arrive at our goal. He is the "Way" because he is the Word made flesh, the perfect Man. The conciliar text continues: "Adam, the first man, was a type of him who was to come, Christ the Lord. Christ the new Adam, in the very revelation of the mystery of the Father and of his love, fully reveals man to himself and brings to light his highest calling."[26] Christ alone, through his humanity, reveals the totality of the mystery of man. Indeed, it is only possible to explore the deeper meaning of this mystery if we take as our starting point man's creation in the image and likeness of God. Man cannot understand himself completely with reference to other visible creatures. The key to his self-understanding lies in contemplating the divine Prototype, the Word made flesh, the eternal Son of the Father. The primary and definitive source for studying the intimate nature of the human being is, therefore, the Most Holy Trinity. The Biblical expression "image and likeness" from the opening pages of the Book of Genesis (cf. Gn 1:26–27) points toward this. So for an in-depth account of the essence of man, we must return to that source.

The constitution *Gaudium et Spes* continues to develop this theme. Christ "is the 'image of the invisible God' (Col 1:15). He is the perfect man who has restored in the children of Adam that likeness to God which had been disfigured ever since the first sin. Human nature, by the very fact that it was assumed, not absorbed, in him, has been raised in us also to a dignity beyond compare."[27] The element of dignity is very important, not to say essential, for Christian anthropology. It affects every branch of the discipline, not only the theoretical aspects but practical matters as well, such as moral teaching, and even documents of political character. The dignity proper to man, according to the teaching of the Council, is based not simply on human nature, but even more on the fact that, in Jesus Christ, God truly became man. The Council text continues: "By his incarnation, he, the Son of God, has in a certain way united himself with each man. He worked with human hands, he thought with a human mind. He acted with a human will, and with a human heart he loved. Born of the Virgin Mary, he has truly been made one of us, like to us in all things except sin."[28] These formulations are the fruit of the Church's profound doctrinal reflection during the first millennium, concerning the correct way to speak of the mystery of the Incarnate God. The question was addressed by almost all the Councils, which continually return to different aspects of this fundamental mystery of faith. The Second Vatican Council bases its teaching on the great wealth of earlier doctrinal reflection on Christ's divine humanity, so as to draw forth a conclusion that is essential for Christian anthropology. This is where its innovative character lies.

The mystery of the Incarnate Word helps us to understand the mystery of man, including his historical dimension. Christ, in fact, is the new Adam, as Saint Paul teaches in the First Letter to the Corinthians (cf. 15:45). The new Adam is man's Redeemer, the Redeemer of the first Adam, that is, of historical man, burdened by the consequences of original sin. To quote once again from *Gaudium et Spes*:

As an innocent lamb he merited life for us by his blood, which he freely shed. In him God reconciled us to himself and to one another, freeing us from the bondage of the devil and of sin, so that each one of us could say with the apostle: the Son of God 'loved me and gave himself for me' (Gal 2:20). By suffering for us he not only gave us an example so that we might follow in his footsteps, but he also opened up a way. If we follow this path, life and death are made holy and acquire a new meaning. . . . The Christian is certainly bound both by need and by duty to struggle with evil through many afflictions and to suffer death; but, as one who has been made a partner in the Paschal Mystery, and as one who has been configured to the death of Christ, he will go forward, strengthened by hope, to the resurrection.[29]

It is said that the Council brought about what Karl Rahner has called the "anthropological revolution." This is a valid insight, but it should be remembered that the revolution was profoundly Christological in character. The anthropology of the Second Vatican Council is rooted in Christology, and therefore in theology. Attentive study of the passage quoted above from the constitution *Gaudium et Spes* takes us to the very heart of the revolution that took place in the Church's approach to anthropology. On the basis of this teaching, I stated in the encyclical *Redemptor Hominis* that "man is the way for the Church."[30]

Gaudium et Spes emphasizes that the explanation of the mystery of man, rooted as it is in the mystery of the Incarnate Word, "holds true not for Christians only but also for all men of good will in whose hearts grace is active invisibly. For since Christ died for all, and since all men are in fact called to one and the same destiny, which is divine, we must hold that the Holy Spirit offers to all the possibility of being made partners, in a way known to God, in the Paschal Mystery."[31]

The Council's anthropology has a markedly dynamic character: it speaks of man in the light of his vocation; it speaks of him existentially. Once again that vision of the mystery of man is proposed which was made known to believers through Christian Revelation.

> Through and in Christ, light is thrown on the riddle of suffering and death which, apart from his Gospel, overwhelms us. Christ has risen again, destroying death by his death, and has given life abundantly to us so that, becoming sons in the Son, we may cry out in the Spirit: Abba, Father![32]

This understanding of the central mystery of Christianity responds directly to the challenges of contemporary thought, which has a similarly existentialist orientation. In modern thought, the key question is about the meaning of human existence, particularly the meaning of suffering and death. From this perspective, the Gospel reveals itself as the supreme prophecy. It is prophecy regarding man. Without the Gospel, man remains a dramatic question with no adequate answer. The correct response to the question about man is Christ, *Redemptor Hominis.*

19. The Mission of the Church

In October 1978 Your Holiness left Poland, so sorely tried by the war and communism, and you came to Rome to become the Successor of Peter. Your Polish experiences brought you closer to a new post-conciliar form of Church: more open to the problems of the laity and the world than in the past. Holy Father, what do you consider to be the most important tasks facing the Church in today's world? What approach should the hierarchy take?

Today an enormous amount of work is needed on the part of the Church. In particular, the lay apostolate is needed, as the Second Vatican Council reminds us. It is absolutely essential to develop a strong sense of mission. The Church in Europe and in every continent has to recognize that it is always and everywhere a missionary Church (*in statu missionis*). The mission belongs so much to its nature that at no time and in no place, not even in countries of long-established Christian tradition, can the Church be other than missionary. This sense of mission, renewed by the Second Vatican Council, was further promoted by Pope Paul VI throughout the fifteen years of his pontificate, with the help of the Synod of Bishops. Hence the apostolic exhortation *Evangelii nuntiandi,* in which Pope Paul spoke from the heart. From the first weeks of my own pontificate, I sought to continue along the same path, as my first document, the encyclical *Redemptor Hominis,* can testify.

In this mission, received from Christ, the Church must work tirelessly. She must be humble and courageous, like Christ himself and his Apostles. If she encounters obstacles, if she is criticized in various ways — maybe accused of so-called proselytism or of trying to clericalize social life — she should not be discouraged. Most of all, she should not cease to proclaim the Gospel. Saint Paul was already aware of this when he wrote to his disciple: "Proclaim the message, be persistent whether the time is favorable or unfavorable, convince, rebuke, and encourage, with the utmost patience in teaching" (2 Tim 4:2). Saint Paul testifies to another urgent inner imperative when he says: "Woe to me if I do not proclaim the

Gospel!" (1 Cor 9:16). Where does this conviction come from? Clearly it comes from recognizing that no other name has been given to us under heaven through which men can be saved, apart from the name of Christ (cf. Acts 4:12).

"Christ yes, the Church no!" is the protest heard from some of our contemporaries. Despite the negative element, this stance appears to show a certain openness toward Christ, which the Enlightenment excluded. Yet it is only an appearance of openness. Christ, if he is truly accepted, is inseparable from the Church, which is his Mystical Body. There is no Christ without the Incarnation; there is no Christ without the Church. The Incarnation of the Son of God in a human body is prolonged, in accordance with his will, in the community of human beings that he constituted, guaranteeing his constant presence among them: "And remember, I am with you always, to the end of the age" (Mt 28:20). Admittedly, the Church, as a human institution, is continually in need of purification and renewal: the Second Vatican Council acknowledged this with courageous candor.[33] Yet the Church, as the Body of Christ, is the normal locus for the presence and action of Christ in the world.

It could be said that these ideas directly or indirectly express the thinking behind the initiatives adopted for the celebration of the second millennium of Christ's birth and the launching of the third. I spoke of this in the two apostolic letters I wrote at that time to the Church and, in a sense, to all people of good will. Both in *Tertio Millennio Adveniente* and in *Novo Millennio Ineunte* I stressed that the Great Jubilee concerned the entire human race to an unprecedented degree. Christ belongs to the history of all humanity, and he gives shape to that history. He brings it to life as only he can, like the yeast in the Gospel. From all eternity God's plan has been to accomplish in Christ the divinization of man and of the world. And this process is continually unfolding — even in our own day.

The image of the Church presented by the dogmatic constitution *Lumen Gentium* needed in some way to be completed. John XXIII himself wisely sensed this, when, in the last weeks before his death, he decided that the Council would prepare a special document concerning the Church in the modern world. This task proved to be extremely fruitful. The constitution *Gaudium et Spes* expressed the Church's openness to the whole content of the concept of "world." In Sacred Scripture, of course, this word has a dual meaning. When, for example, the sacred authors speak of the "spirit of this world" (cf. 1 Cor 2:12), they mean everything in the world that separates us from God: today we would express this under the heading of secularization. Yet this negative meaning of "world" in Scripture is balanced by the positive meaning: the world as God's creation, the world as the sum of the goods that the Creator has given to man, entrusting them to him as a task to be completed with initiative, insight, and responsibility. The world, which is like the theater of man's history, bears the marks of his travail, his triumphs, and his failures. Damaged by man's sin, it has been redeemed by Christ crucified and risen, and now, with man's active cooperation, awaits its glorious fulfilment.[34] Paraphrasing the words of Saint Irenaeus, one might say: *Gloria Dei — mundus secundum amorem Dei ab homine excultus* — the glory of God is the world perfected by man according to God's love.

20. The Relationship Between Church and State

The Church's missionary activity is always carried out in a particular society and in the territory of a particular State. Holy Father, how do you see the relationship between Church and State in our present situation?

The constitution *Gaudium et Spes* has this to say:

The political community and the Church are autonomous and independent of each other in their own fields. Nevertheless, both are devoted to the personal vocation of man, though under different titles. This service will redound the more effectively to the welfare of all insofar as both institutions practice better cooperation according to the local and prevailing situation. For man's horizons are not bounded only by the temporal order; living on the level of human history he preserves the integrity of his eternal destiny.[35]

The way the Council understands the term "separation" of Church and State is far removed from the way totalitarian systems interpreted it. It came as a surprise and, in a certain sense, also as a challenge for several countries, particularly those under Communist rule. Clearly, these regimes could not disagree with the Council's position, but at the same time they realized that it was at odds with their notion of separation of Church and State. According to their vision, the world belongs exclusively to the State; the Church has its own sphere, which lies beyond the "boundaries," so to speak, of the world. The conciliar vision of the Church "in" the world conflicts with that interpretation. For the Church, the world is both a task and a challenge. It is so for all Christians, but particularly for the lay faithful. The Council gave prominence to the question of the lay apostolate, that is, the active presence of Christians in the life of society. Yet according to Marxist ideology, this was precisely the area where it was necessary to establish exclusive control by the State and the party.

This is worth pointing out, because there are political parties today which, despite their firm democratic credentials, demonstrate a growing tendency to interpret the separation of Church and State according to the Communist model. Naturally, today's society has the means to defend itself. Yet society must have the will to do so. And it is in this area that a certain passivity in the attitude of believing citizens gives cause for concern. It seems as if their sense of their religious rights was keener in the past, when they were readier to defend them through the democratic means at their disposal. Today such reactions are much more muted and have virtually gone into abeyance, perhaps partly because of insufficient preparation of the political elite.

In the twentieth century great efforts were made to stop people believing, to make them reject Christ. Toward the end of the century, the end of the millennium, those destructive forces were weakened, yet they left a trail of devastation behind them. I am speaking of a devastation of consciences, with ruinous consequences in the moral sphere, affecting personal and social morality and the mores of family life. Pastors of souls, who engage every day with the spiritual lives of their flocks, know this better than anyone. When I have occasion to speak with them, I often hear disturbing admissions. Sadly, one could describe Europe at the dawn of the new millennium as a continent of devastation. Political programs, aimed principally at economic development, are not enough to heal wounds of this nature. On the contrary, they could even make them worse. Here an enormous task opens up for the Church. The evangelical harvest in today's world is great indeed. We have only to ask the Lord, and to ask insistently, that he send laborers for this harvest that is ready and waiting to be reaped.

21. Europe in the Context of Other Continents

Holy Father, perhaps it would be helpful to consider Europe from the point of view of its relationship with other continents. You yourself took part in the work of the Council and you have met many people from all over the world, especially during your numerous apostolic journeys. What impressions have you formed from these encounters?

I shall speak principally of my experience as a Bishop, both during the Council itself and in the years that followed, in the course of my work with the different dicasteries of the Roman Curia. Particularly important for me was the experience of taking part in the Assemblies of the Synod of Bishops. These various encounters allowed me to form a fairly accurate picture of the relationships between Europe and non-European countries, especially non-European Churches. The relationships took shape, in the light of conciliar teaching, in terms of the *communio ecclesiarum,* a communion consisting of an exchange of goods and services, leading to mutual enrichment. The Catholic Church in Europe, especially in Western Europe, has lived for centuries alongside Christians of the Reformation; in the East the Orthodox are in the majority. The most Catholic continent outside Europe is Latin America. In North America Catholics constitute a relative majority. The situation in Australia and Oceania is quite similar. In the Philippines, most people belong to the Church, but in Asia overall, Catholics form a minority. Africa is a missionary continent, where the Church continues to grow significantly. Most non-European Churches were established by missionaries who set out from Europe. Today these Churches have their own identity and a definite character. Whereas in the past the Church in North and South America, in Africa, and in Asia, could be considered a European "export," de facto they now constitute a kind of spiritual counterweight for the Old Continent, the more so inasmuch as a certain process of dechristianization is taking place there.

The twentieth century has been marked by rivalry between the three "worlds." The meaning of this phrase is well known:

during the Communist domination of Eastern Europe, the area behind the iron curtain, the "collectivist" world, came to be known as the Second World in contrast to the capitalist First World, made up of the West. Everywhere else was known as the Third World, alluding, in particular, to developing countries.

In such a divided world, the Church quickly realized that she needed to develop a varied approach to her task of evangelization. With regard to social justice, a vital element of evangelization, the Church continued to promote just progress among the peoples of the capitalist world, yet without yielding to the processes of dechristianization rooted in the old Enlightenment traditions. In her dealings with the Second World, the Communist world, the Church sensed the urgency of aligning herself, above all, with the defense of human rights and the rights of nations. This applied not only to Poland, but also to neighboring countries. Finally, in Third World countries, as well as introducing Christianity to the people, the Church took it upon herself to draw attention to the unjust distribution of goods, not only between different social groupings but between different regions of the world. In fact, the gap became increasingly evident between the rich North, which was growing richer, and the poor South, which continued to be exploited and penalized in many ways even after the end of the colonial era. Instead of diminishing, the poverty of the South was constantly increasing. Such are the consequences of unbridled capitalism, which makes the rich ever richer while forcing the poor into conditions of growing degradation.

This is the vision of Europe's place in the world that I gained from my contacts with the Bishops of other continents during and after the Council. After my election to the See of Peter, on October 16, 1978, I was able to confirm this vision and explore it further, both here in Rome and on my pastoral visits to different Churches all over the world. This vision has informed the way I have conducted my ministry of evangelization in a world which for the most part has already heard the Gospel. During these years I have always tried to devote particular care to those activities which bring the Church into dialogue with the modern world. The constitution *Gaudium et Spes* speaks of the "world," but this term actually denotes a range of different worlds. I spoke of this during the Council, when I made my intervention as Metropolitan of Kraków.

DEMOCRACY: POSSIBILITIES AND RISKS

22. Modern Democracy

The French Revolution spread throughout the world the slogan "liberty, equality, fraternity," the program of modern democracy. Holy Father, what is your evaluation of the democratic system in its current Western form?

Our reflections so far have led us to consider a question which seems particularly significant for European civilization: it is the question of democracy, understood not only as a political system but also as an attitude of mind and a principle of conduct. Democracy is rooted in Greek tradition, although in ancient Greece it did not have the exact meaning it has acquired in modern times. The classical distinction between the three possible forms of political regime is well known: monarchy, aristocracy, and democracy. Each of these systems gives its own answer to the question about the primary subject of power. In a monarchical system, the subject is an individual, whether he be king, emperor, or sovereign prince. In an aristocratic system the subject is a social group which exercises power on the basis of particular titles of merit such as, for example, prowess in battle, lineage, wealth. In a democratic system, however, the subject of power is the whole society, the "people," *demos* in Greek. Obviously the direct exercise of power by all is impossible, so the democratic form of government depends on the work of representatives of the people, designated through free elections.

All three ways of exercising power have existed in the course of history, and all three continue to exist today, despite the modern trend which decisively favors the democratic system as the one which best corresponds to the rational and social nature of man and, specifically, to the demands of social justice. In fact, it is hard not to acknowledge that, if society is made up of men and every man is a social being, everyone should be allowed to participate in power, even if indirectly.

If we consider Polish history, it is possible to observe the gradual transition from one to another of these three political systems, and also their progressive interpenetration. If the State of the Piast was clearly monarchical in character, from the time of the

Jagiellonians the monarchy became more and more constitutional; when that dynasty died out, the government, while still monarchical, came to depend on an oligarchy composed of the nobility. Yet since the nobility was quite extensive, it was necessary to have recourse to a form of democratic election of those who would represent the nobles. This led to a kind of democracy among the nobility. Thus did a constitutional monarchy coexist with democracy among the nobility for several centuries within a single State. While at first this was one of the strengths of the Polish-Lithuanian-Ruthenian State, the passage of time and changing circumstances brought to light more and more imbalances and weaknesses in the system, which eventually led to the loss of independence.

When it regained its liberty, the Polish Republic was established as a democratic state with a president and a bicameral parliament. After the fall of the so-called People's Republic of Poland in 1989, the Third Republic returned to a system similar to that which had existed before the Second World War. As for the period of the People's Poland, it must be said that, despite the label of "people's democracy," power lay de facto in the hands of the Communist party (a party oligarchy): the first secretary of the party was at the same time the country's political leader.

This brief sketch of the history of different forms of government allows us to arrive at a better evaluation of the democratic credentials of a system according to the criteria of social ethics. While in monarchical and oligarchical systems (for example, the Polish democracy of the nobility), one part of society (often the vast majority) is condemned to a passive or subordinate role, because power is concentrated in the hands of a few; this ought not to happen in democratic regimes. Does it really not happen? Certain situations which can arise in democracies justify the question. Catholic social ethics favor the democratic solution in principle, because it corresponds more closely, as I mentioned earlier, to the rational and social nature of man. Yet it is important to add that we are still a long way from "canonizing" this system. Each of the possible solutions — monarchy, aristocracy, and democracy — can, in certain conditions, help to achieve the essential purpose of exercising power, that is to say, to serve the common good. An indispensable presupposition for any solution, though, is respect for fundamental ethical norms. Politics is simply social ethics, as Aristotle recognized. This means that civic virtues have to be exercised if a given system of government is not to turn corrupt. Greek tradition gave a name to the degeneration of each of the systems mentioned. That of the monarchy was known as tyranny, while for pathological forms of democracy Polybius coined the term "ochlocracy," that is to say, domination by the populace.

After the collapse of the ideologies of the twentieth century, and especially after the fall of communism, various nations pinned their hopes on democracy. Yet we need to ask ourselves what a democracy ought to be. It is often said that with democracy, the true State of law is realized. In this system, in fact, social life is regulated by laws established by parliaments with legislative power. In these assemblies, norms are drawn up which delimit the conduct of citizens in the various areas of social life. Every area clearly requires legislation that will ensure its ordered development. In this way a State of law accomplishes the purpose of every democracy: that of forming a society of free citizens who jointly pursue the common good.

That said, it may be helpful to return to the history of Israel. I have already spoken of Abraham as the one who put his faith in God's promises; he trustingly accepted his word and thereby became the father of many nations. From this point of view, it is significant that both Jews and Christians look to Abraham as their father. So do Muslims. Yet the basis of the State of Israel as an organized society came not from Abraham but from Moses. It was Moses who led his fellow Israelites out of the land of Egypt, and in the course of their journey through the desert he authoritatively established a State of law in the Biblical sense of the word. This is something worth underlining: Israel, as God's chosen people, was a theocratic society, in which Moses was not only the charismatic leader but also the prophet. His task, in God's name, was to build the juridical and religious foundations for the people's common life. A key moment in this work was the event which took place at the foot of Mount Sinai. There, the Covenant was established between God and the people of Israel on the basis of the Law given by God to Moses on the mountain. Essentially, the Law consisted of the Decalogue: the ten commandments, the ten principles of conduct, without which no human community, no nation, not even the international community, can function.

The commandments, carved on two stone tablets which Moses received on Sinai, are also inscribed on human hearts. Saint Paul tells us this in the Letter to the Romans: "What the law requires is written on their hearts, to which their own conscience also bears witness" (2:15). The divine law of the Decalogue is also binding, as natural law, for those who do not accept Revelation: do not kill, do not commit adultery, do not steal, do not bear false witness, honor your father and your mother . . . Each of these commands from the Sinai code seeks to defend a fundamental good of human and social life. If such a law is placed in doubt, ordered human society becomes impossible and man's moral existence is put at risk. Moses is not the author of the tablets of the Commandments which he brought down from the mountain. Rather, he is the servant and the spokesman of the Law given to him by God on Sinai. He goes on to formulate a highly detailed code of conduct based on this Law, which he consigns to the sons and daughters of Israel in the Pentateuch.

Christ confirmed the commandments of the Decalogue as the foundation of Christian morals, synthesizing them in the twin precepts of love of God and love of neighbor. And he gives a truly comprehensive interpretation of the term "neighbor" in the Gospel. The love to which the Christian is committed embraces everyone, including enemies. When I was writing the essay *Love and Responsibility*, the greatest commandment of the Gospel presented itself to me as a personalist norm. Precisely because man is a personal being, it is not possible to fulfil our duty toward him except by loving him. Just as love is the supreme commandment with regard to the personal God, so too only love can be our fundamental obligation toward the human person, created in God's image and likeness.

It is this moral code, coming from God and sanctioned in both Old and New Covenants, which is also the intangible basis of all human legislation in any system, particularly a democratic system. The law established by man, by parliaments, and by every other human legislator must not contradict the natural law, that is to say, the eternal law of God. Saint Thomas gave us this famous definition of law: *Lex est quaedam rationis ordinatio ad bonum commune, ab eo qui curam communitatis habet promulgata* — the law is a rational ordering promulgated for the sake of the common good by him who has the care of the community.[36] As a "rational ordering," law rests on the truth of being: the truth of God, the truth of man, the truth of all created reality. That truth is the basis of natural law. To this the legislator adds the act of promulgation. For God's Law this happened on Sinai, and for modern legislation it happens in parliaments.

Let us now consider a question of great importance to the history of Europe in the twentieth century. It was a regularly elected parliament that consented to Hitler's rise to power in Germany in the 1930s. And the same Reichstag, by delegating full powers to Hitler (*Ermächtigungsgesetz*), paved the way for his policy of invading Europe, for the establishment of concentration camps, and for the implementation of the so-called "final solution" to the Jewish question, that is to say, the elimination of millions of the sons and daughters of Israel. Suffice it to recall these events, so close to us in time, in order to see clearly that law established by man has definite limits, which it must not overstep. They are the limits determined by the law of nature, through which God himself safeguards man's fundamental good. Hitler's crimes had their Nuremberg, where those responsible were judged and punished by human justice. In many cases, however, this element is lacking, even if there always

189

remains the supreme judgment of the Divine Legislator. A profound mystery surrounds the manner in which Justice and Mercy meet in God when he judges men and their history.

From this perspective, as we enter a new century and a new millennium, we must question certain legislative choices made by the parliaments of today's democratic regimes. The most immediate example concerns abortion laws. When a parliament authorizes the termination of pregnancy, agreeing to the elimination of the unborn child, it commits a grave abuse against an innocent human being utterly unable to defend itself. Parliaments which approve and promulgate such laws must be aware that they are exceeding their proper competence and placing themselves in open conflict with God's law and the law of nature.

23. Back to Europe?

A highly topical question concerns Poland's relationship with the new Europe. One might ask what traditional links exist between Poland and modern Western Europe. Could difficulties arise from its recent entry into European institutions? Holy Father, how do you see the place and the role of Poland within Europe?

After the fall of communism, a number of voices were heard in Poland in support of the thesis that the nation needed to re-enter Europe. There were certainly good reasons for expressing it in this way. Clearly, the totalitarian system imposed from the East had separated us from Europe. The so-called "iron curtain" had been an eloquent symbol of this. From other points of view, however, the thesis of the "return to Europe," even in relation to the most recent period of our history, did not appear correct. Although politically separated from the rest of the Continent, the Poles spared no efforts in those years to make their proper contribution to the formation of the new Europe. How can we forget their heroic struggle in 1939 against the Nazi aggressor and then, in 1944, the uprising in Warsaw against the horrors of the occupation? Another significant development was that of *Solidarność*, which led to the fall of the totalitarian system in the East — not only in Poland, but also in neighboring countries. So it is hard to accept without further clarification the thesis that Poland "had to return to Europe." She was already in Europe, having actively participated in its formation. I have spoken of this on numerous occasions, protesting against the injustice that has been done to Poland and to the Poles by the misleading thesis of a "return" to Europe.

This protest led me to take another look at Polish history, in order to find out what contribution Poland has made to the formation of the so-called "European spirit." It is a contribution which began centuries ago at the time of the "baptism of Poland," particularly at the Congress of Gniezno in the year 1000. Receiving baptism from neighboring Bohemia, the first sovereigns of the Piast Kingdom of Poland chose to establish a new political entity in that part of Europe; despite its historical weaknesses, the nation has proved able to survive and to serve as a bastion against various external pressures.

So we Poles were involved in the formation of Europe. We contributed to the course of its history and we fought to defend it from aggression. Suffice it to recall, for example, the Battle of Legnica (1241), when Poland halted the Mongol invasion of Europe.[37] Then there was the whole issue of the Teutonic Order, which came to the attention of the Council of Constance (1414–1418).[38] Yet Poland's contribution was not purely military. On the cultural level too, she had a significant impact on the formation of Europe. In this area, credit is often given to the School of Salamanca, and in particular to the Spanish Dominican Francisco de Vitoria (1492–1546), for drawing up international law, and rightly so. Yet it should not be forgotten that earlier still, the Pole Paweł Włodkowic (1370–1435) proclaimed those same principles as the basis for the orderly coexistence of peoples. Conversion not with the sword but with persuasion — *Plus ratio quam vis* — is the golden rule of the Jagiellonian University, which has done so much to promote European culture. This university witnessed the activity of such eminent scholars as Mateusz of Kraków (1330–1410) and Nicolaus Copernicus (1473–1543). Another important fact should be mentioned: at a time when Western Europe was seething with the wars of religion that followed the Reformation, wars to which a misguided solution was applied by means of the principle *cuius regio eius religio,* the last of the Jagiellonians, Sigismund Augustus, solemnly declared: "I am not the king of your consciences." In Poland there were no wars of religion. Instead there was a tendency to seek accords and unions. Politically, there was the union with Lithuania; ecclesially, the Union of Brest was agreed toward the end of the sixteenth century between the Catholic Church and Eastern-rite Christians. Although little is known about all this in the West, it clearly indicates an essential contribution to the formation of Europe's Christian spirit. Hence the sixteenth century is rightly called Poland's "golden age."

The seventeenth century, on the other hand, especially the second half, saw the beginnings of a crisis both in the political sphere, at home and abroad, and in the religious sphere. From this point of view, the defense of Jasna Góra in 1655[39] not only seemed like a historical miracle but could also be interpreted as a warning for the future: it drew attention to the danger coming from the West, dominated by the principle *cuius regio eius religio,* and also from the East, where Tsarist autocracy was being consolidated more and more. In the light of all this, it could be said that if the Poles have a fault vis-à-vis Europe and the European spirit, it is that they allowed the magnificent heritage of the fifteenth and sixteenth centuries to perish.

The eighteenth century was a time of profound decadence. The Poles permitted the patrimony of the Jagiellonians, of Báthory, and of John Sobieski III, to be destroyed. It must not be forgotten that, toward the end of the seventeenth century, it was John Sobieski III who saved Europe from the Ottoman threat at the battle of Vienna (1683). His victory removed that particular danger from Europe for a long time. Here, history was in a sense repeating itself, reliving what had happened in the thirteenth century at the Battle of Legnica. The mistake the Poles made in the eighteenth century was that they failed to safeguard that heritage, whose ultimate champion was the victor of Vienna. It is well known that Poland was entrusted to the Saxon dynasty as a result of external pressures, especially on the part of Russia, which wanted to destroy not only the Republic of Poland but also the values it embodied. In the course of the eighteenth century, the Poles were unable to halt this process of decay, or to defend themselves against the destructive influence of the *liberum veto*.[40] The nobles failed to restore the legitimate rights of the third estate or of the great multitudes of peasants; they failed to liberate them from serfdom and render them responsible citizens of the Republic. These were serious mistakes made by the nobility, especially by a good part of the aristocracy, by State dignitaries and, unfortunately, also by some Church dignitaries.

In this examination of conscience regarding our contribution to Europe, then, we have to devote particular attention to our eighteenth-century history. On the one hand, this allows us to acknowledge the full extent of the mistakes and failures of that time, but, on the other hand, it also encourages us to note the beginnings of a renewal. For example, let us not forget the Commission for National Education, the first attempts at armed resistance to the invaders and, especially, the great work of the Diet of Four Years.[41] The burden of our mistakes and failures outweighed these things, and it crushed Poland. Yet in falling, she brought with her, as if in a testament, seeds of rebirth that would lead to the recovery of independence and to Poland's later contribution to the building of Europe. This new chapter would begin only after the nineteenth-century regimes and the so-called "Holy Alliance" had fallen.

With the recovery of independence in 1918, Poland could once again participate actively in the formation of Europe. Thanks to some leading politicians and eminent economists, it was possible to attain significant results in a short space of time. To tell the truth, in the West, especially in Great Britain, Poland was viewed with suspicion. Yet with each passing year she showed herself to be a reliable contributor to postwar Europe. And she was a courageous contributor, as became clear in 1939: while the Western democracies deluded themselves into thinking they could achieve something by negotiating with Hitler, Poland chose to accept the war, despite the clear inferiority of her military and technological forces. At that moment the Polish authorities judged that this was the only way to defend the future of Europe and the European spirit.

On the evening of October 16, 1978, when I appeared at the balcony of Saint Peter's Basilica to greet the people of Rome and the pilgrims gathered on the piazza, waiting for the result of the conclave, I said that I came "from a far country." In fact, the geographical distance is not great. By air the journey takes barely two hours. In calling it a "far country" I intended to allude to the presence of the "iron curtain." The Pope from behind the iron curtain truly came from afar, even if, in reality, he came from the very center of Europe. The geographical center of the Continent is actually located on Polish territory.

During the iron curtain years, Central Europe was almost forgotten. The division between East and West was applied rather mechanically; this was aptly symbolized by Berlin, the capital of Germany, which belonged partly to West Germany and partly to East Germany. In reality, the division was quite artificial. It served political and military purposes. It established the boundaries of the two blocs, but it did not take account of the history of the peoples concerned. For the Poles it was unacceptable to be described as a people of the East, partly because the nation's boundaries, in those very years, had moved farther West. I imagine that it was equally difficult for the Czechs, the Slovaks, and the Hungarians to accept this label, to say nothing of the Lithuanians, Latvians, and Estonians.

From this point of view, to summon a Pope from Poland, from Kraków, could serve as an eloquent symbol. It was not simply the summons of an individual, but of the entire Church to which he belonged since birth; indirectly, it was also a call to his nation. It seems to me that Cardinal Stefan Wyszyński saw and expressed this aspect of the event in a particularly profound way. Personally I have always been convinced that the election of a Polish Pope can be explained in terms of all that the Primate of the Millennium had achieved, along with the rest of the Episcopate and the Polish Church, despite the oppressive limitations and persecutions to which they were subjected in those difficult years.

In sending the Apostles to the furthest ends of the earth, Christ said to them: "You will be my witnesses" (Acts 1:8). All Christians are called to be witnesses of Christ. In a particular way the pastors of the Church are so called. By electing a Cardinal from Poland to the See of Rome, the conclave was making a significant choice: it was as if they wanted to call upon the witness of the Church from which that Cardinal came — and to call upon it for the good of the Universal Church. In any case, their choice had a particular significance for Europe and for the world. By a tradition lasting almost five centuries, the responsibility of the See of Peter had devolved upon an Italian Cardinal. The election of a Pole seemed like a revolution. It demonstrated that the conclave, following the indications of the Council, was seeking to read the "signs of the times" and to ponder its decisions in the light of these.

In this context, we might usefully reflect on the contribution that Central and Eastern Europe can make today to the formation of a united Europe. I have spoken about this on numerous occasions. It seems to me that the most important contribution the countries of that region can offer is to defend their identity. The nations of Central and Eastern Europe have preserved their identity, and even consolidated it, despite all that was imposed upon them by the Communist dictators. For them, the fight to preserve national identity was a fight for survival. Today the two parts of Europe — East and West — are coming closer together. This phenomenon, positive in itself, is not without risk. The principal danger facing Eastern Europe today seems to me to be the weakening of its identity. During the struggle against Marxist totalitarianism, that part of Europe went through a process of spiritual maturation, thanks to which certain values essential for human life have not declined there as much as in the West. In Eastern Europe, for example, there is still a strong conviction that God is the supreme guarantor of human dignity and human rights. So where does the risk lie? It lies in an uncritical submission to the influence of negative cultural models, widespread in the West. For Central and Eastern Europe, where such tendencies can seem like a kind of "cultural progress," this is one of the most serious challenges today. This, I am convinced, is the area where a great spiritual confrontation is taking place, the outcome of which will determine the face of the new Europe being formed at the start of the millennium.

In 1994, at Castel Gandolfo, a symposium was held on the theme of the identity of European societies (*Identity in Change*). The discussion focused on the changes brought about by the events of the twentieth century in the way European identity and national identity are understood in the context of modern civilization. At the beginning of the symposium, Paul Ricœur spoke of remembering and forgetting as two important and mutually opposed forces that operate in human and social history. Memory is the faculty which models the identity of human beings at both a personal and a collective level. In fact, it is through memory that our sense of identity forms and defines itself in the personal psyche. Among the many interesting things I heard on that occasion, this struck me particularly. Christ was acquainted with this law of memory and he invoked it at the key moment of his mission. When he was instituting the Eucharist during the Last Supper, he said: "Do this in memory of me" (*Hoc facite in meam commemorationem;* Lk 22:19). Memory evokes recollections. The Church is, in a certain sense, the "living memory" of Christ: of the mystery of Christ, of his Passion, death, and resurrection, of his Body and Blood. This "memory" is accomplished through the Eucharist. It follows that Christians, as they celebrate the Eucharist in "memory" of their Master, continually discover their own identity. The Eucharist highlights something more profound and at the same time more universal — it highlights the divinization of man and the new creation in Christ. It speaks of the redemption of the world. This memory of the redemption and divinization of man, so profound and so universal, also triggers many other dimensions of memory, both personal and collective. It allows man to understand himself deeply, within the definitive perspective of his humanity. It allows him to understand the different communities in which his history evolves: the family, the clan, the nation. Finally, it allows him to understand the history of language and culture, the history of all that is true, good, and beautiful.

24. The Maternal Memory of the Church

In recent decades in various parts of the world, enormous changes have taken place and much has been said about the need for the Church to adapt to new cultural realities. The urgent question of the Church's identity also arises. How would you define the elements of this identity, Holy Father?

In order to answer this question, it is helpful to consider it from another angle. In describing the events of Jesus's infancy, Saint Luke says: "His mother treasured all these things in her heart" (Lk 2:51). This refers to her recollection of his words and of the events surrounding the incarnation of the Son of God. Mary preserved in her heart the memory of the mystery of the Annunciation, because that was the moment when the Incarnate Word was conceived in her womb (cf. Jn 1:14). She preserved the memory of those months when the Word was hidden within her. Then came the moment of Our Lord's birth with all that went with it. Mary remembered how Jesus was born in Bethlehem: since there was no room in the inn, he entered the world in a stable (cf. Lk 2:7). Yet his birth occurred amid supernatural signs: shepherds in nearby fields came to pay homage to the Child (cf. Lk 2:15–17); later in Bethlehem, the Magi came from the East (cf. Mt 2:1–12); then, together with Saint Joseph, Mary had to flee to Egypt to save her son from Herod's wrath (cf. Mt 2:13–15). All this was faithfully recorded in Mary's memory and we may reasonably conclude that she passed it on to Saint Luke, who was particularly close to her. She also passed it on to Saint John, to whom Jesus had entrusted her at the hour of his death.

It is true that John summarizes the entire infancy narrative in a single phrase: "And the Word became flesh and lived among us" (Jn 1:14), framing this simple statement with the magnificent Prologue of his Gospel. Yet it is also true that only in John do we find an account of the first miracle worked by Jesus, at his mother's request (cf. Jn 2:1–11). And it is John again, and he alone, who recounts the words with which Jesus, at the hour of his agony, entrusted his mother to him (cf. Jn 19:26–27). We may presume that Mary preserved all these events carved indelibly in her memory. "His mother treasured all these things in her heart" (Lk 2:51).

Mary's memory is a source of singular importance for knowing Christ, an incomparable source. Mary is not only a witness to the mystery of the Incarnation, in which she knowingly cooperated. She also followed step-by-step the gradual self-revelation of her Son as he was growing up beside her. The Gospel stories are familiar. The twelve-year-old Jesus tells Mary of the special mission he has received from the Father (cf. Lk 2:49). Later, when he leaves Nazareth, his mother always remains in some way associated with him: this becomes clear from the miracle at Cana in Galilee (cf. Jn 2:1–11) and elsewhere (cf. Mk 3:31–35; Mt 12:46–50; Lk 8:19–21). In particular, Mary was to witness the mystery of the Passion and its fulfilment on Calvary (cf. Jn 19:25–27). Even if there is no mention of it in the Biblical texts, it is conceivable that she was the first to whom the Risen Lord appeared. In any event, Mary was present at his Ascension into heaven, she was with the Apostles in the Upper Room awaiting the descent of the Holy Spirit, and she was a witness to the birth of the Church on the day of Pentecost.

This maternal memory of Mary is particularly important for the divine-human identity of the Church. It could be said that the memory of the new People of God is intimately associated with Mary's memory, and that the celebration of the Eucharist relives events and teachings of Christ learned from the lips of his mother. Moreover, the Church has a maternal memory of her own, because she herself is a mother, a mother who remembers. The Church, in her turn, safeguards what was present in Mary's memories.

The Church's memory grows as the Church grows, principally through the witness of Apostles and the suffering of martyrs. It is a memory which reveals itself gradually in history, starting from the Acts of the Apostles, but it cannot be totally identified with history. It is something quite specific. The technical term to describe it is Tradition. This word refers to the active function of remembering by handing on. What else is Tradition but the task assumed by the Church of transmitting (in Latin, *tradere*) the mystery of Christ and the entirety of his teaching preserved in her memory? It is a task in which the Church is constantly sustained by the Holy Spirit. During his farewell discourse, Christ speaks to the Apostles of the Holy Spirit: "He will teach you everything and remind you of all that I have said to you" (Jn 14:26). The Church, when she celebrates the Eucharist, which is the "memorial" of the Lord, does so in the power of the Holy Spirit, who from day to day awakens and directs her memory. To this marvelous and mysterious work of the Spirit, the Church, from generation to generation, owes her essential identity. And this has already lasted for two thousand years.

The memory of this fundamental identity, with which Christ endowed his Church, has proved stronger than all the divisions introduced by men into their ecclesial inheritance. At the beginning of the third millennium, Christians, though divided among themselves, are conscious that unity and not division belongs to the most profound essence of the Church. And they are conscious of this by virtue of the words of institution of the Eucharist: "Do this in memory of me" (Lk 22:19). These are univocal words; words which admit neither divisions nor schisms.

This unity of memory accompanies the Church from generation to generation as history runs its course, and it expresses itself particularly in Mary's memory. This happens partly because Mary is a woman. To tell the truth, memory belongs more to the mystery of woman than to that of man. Thus it is in the history of families, in the history of tribes and nations, and thus too in the history of the Church. There are many reasons for the Marian cult in the Church, for the large number of shrines dedicated to Mary in different parts of the world. The Second Vatican Council has this to say about Mary: she "is a type of the Church in the order of faith, charity, and perfect union with Christ. For in the mystery of the Church, which is itself rightly called mother and virgin, the Blessed Virgin stands out in eminent and singular fashion as exemplar both of virgin and mother."[42] Mary led the way because hers is the most faithful memory, or rather, because her memory is the most faithful reflection of the mystery of God, transmitted in her to the Church and through the Church to humanity.

What is at issue here is not only the mystery of Christ. In him, it is the mystery of man that is revealed from the beginning. There is probably no other text on the origins of man so simple and yet so complete as that contained in the first three chapters of the Book of Genesis. Here not only do we find an account of the creation of man as male and female (cf. Gn 1:27), but his particular vocation in the universe is made abundantly clear. In brief but quite transparent terms, we glimpse the truth about man's original state, a state of innocence and happiness, we observe the very different scenario of sin and its effects — what scholastic theology describes as *status naturae lapsae* (the state of fallen nature) — and we learn of the immediate divine initiative pointing to the Redemption (cf. Gn 3:15).

The Church preserves within herself the memory of man's history from the beginning: the memory of his creation, his vocation, his elevation, and his fall. Within this essential framework the whole of human history, the history of Redemption, is written. The Church is a mother who, like Mary, treasures in her heart the story of her children, making all their problems her own.

There was a clear echo of this truth during the Great Jubilee of the Year 2000. The Church celebrated it as a jubilee of the birth of Jesus Christ, but also as a jubilee of man's origins, of man's appearance in the universe, of his elevation, and of his vocation. The constitution *Gaudium et Spes* rightly said that the mystery of man is fully revealed only in Christ:

In reality it is only in the mystery of the Word made flesh that the mystery of man truly becomes clear. Adam, the first man, was a type of him who was to come, Christ the Lord. Christ the new Adam, in the very revelation of the mystery of the Father and of his love, fully reveals man to himself and brings to light his highest calling.[43]

Saint Paul said something similar:

The first man, Adam, became a living being; the last Adam became a life-giving spirit. But it is not the spiritual that is first, but the physical and then the spiritual. The first man was from the earth, a man of dust, the second man is from heaven. As was the man of dust, so are those who are of the dust; and as is the man of heaven, so are those who are of heaven. Just as we have borne the image of the man of dust, we will also bear the image of the man of heaven. (1 Cor 15:45–49)

This was the essential meaning of the Great Jubilee. The occurrence of the year 2000 was important not just for Christianity but for the entire human family. The question about man, which is asked repeatedly, finds its complete answer in Jesus Christ. It could be said that the Great Jubilee of the Year 2000 was the jubilee both of Christ's birth and of the answer to the question about the meaning and sense of being human. And it is linked to the dimension of memory. Mary's memory and the Church's memory enable man to rediscover his true identity at the dawn of the new millennium.

25. The Vertical Dimension of European History

We have arrived at the crucial question concerning man and his destiny: How are we to understand the deepest meaning of history? Is it sufficient to adopt an approach to the question that remains within the limits of time and space?

Human history obviously unfolds in a horizontal dimension within space and time. Yet it also has a vertical dimension. It is not only we who write our history: God writes it with us. This dimension of history, which we might label "transcendent," the Enlightenment decisively rejected. The Church, however, returns to it repeatedly: the Second Vatican Council provides clear evidence of this.

In what way does God write our history? An answer is given in the Bible, from the opening chapters of the Book of Genesis right up to the final pages of the Apocalypse. At the very beginning of human history, God reveals himself as the God of the promise. Such is the God of Abraham, the great patriarch of whom Saint Paul says that he "had faith hoping against hope" (cf. Rom 4:18): he accepted without question God's promise that he would become the father of a great nation. To all appearances, it was an impossible promise: he was, after all, an old man, and his wife, Sarah, had also grown old. Humanly speaking, their hopes of having any descendants seemed non-existent (cf. Gn 18:11–14). And yet a child was born to them. God's promise to Abraham was fulfilled (cf. Gn 21:1–7). The son of his old age was given the name Isaac and from him issued Abraham's descendants, gradually growing into a nation. Israel is God's chosen nation, to whom he promised a Messiah. The entire history of Israel is a time of waiting for God to carry out this promise.

The promise has a specific object: God's "blessing" for Abraham and his descendants. These are the words with which God enters into dialogue with him: "I will make of you a great nation, and I will bless you, and make your name great, so that you will be a blessing . . . by you all the families of the earth shall bless themselves" (Gn 12:2–3). To understand the salvific importance of this promise, we have to go back to the first chapters of the Book of Genesis and, in particular, to the third chapter, where we read of the Lord's conversation with the dramatis personae of the original Fall. God calls first the man and then the woman to account for what they have done. And when the man blames his wife, she in turn points to the tempter (cf. Gn 3:11–13). It was he who had instigated the transgression of God's command (cf. Gn 3:1–5). Yet it is interesting to note that the promise of the future plan of salvation is already contained in the curse addressed by God to the serpent. God curses the evil spirit, the instigator of the original sin of our first parents, but at the same time he utters words that express the first Messianic promise. He says to the serpent: "I will put enmity between you and the woman and between your offspring and hers; he will strike your head, and you will strike his heel" (Gn 3:15). It is a synthetic outline, but it says everything. The promise of salvation is contained here and we already obtain a glimpse of the entire history of humanity as far as the Apocalypse: the woman announced in the Protoevangelium appears in the pages of the Apocalypse clothed with the sun and crowned with twelve stars, while the ancient dragon presses upon her, wishing to devour her offspring (cf. Rv 12:1–6).

Until the end of time, this struggle between good and evil will continue, between the sin inherited from our first parents and the saving grace won by Christ, Son of Mary. He is the fulfillment of the promise made to Abraham and inherited by Israel. With his coming, the last times have begun, the times of eschatological completion. God kept his word to Abraham by making a Covenant with Israel through Moses, and in Christ his Son he opened up to all mankind the prospect of eternal life beyond the end of earthly history. This is man's extraordinary destiny: called to the dignity of an adopted son of God, he accepts this vocation in faith and he commits himself to build up the Kingdom, in which the history of the human race on earth will reach its definitive point of arrival.

In this regard, I am reminded of some verses that I wrote years ago, speaking of man and the God-Man, the incarnate Word of God, in whom alone history acquires its full meaning. I said:

Oh Man, on You I call, for You I
   search
in whom man's history finds its
   body.
I approach you saying, not "Come"

But simply "be."
Be there where not one trace is
    found
but where man once did dwell,
where heart and soul, desire, pain,
    will,
were consumed by emotions ablaze
    with holy shame.
Be as the eternal seismograph of
    things invisible but real.
O Man, in whom are met the
    heights and depths of man,
in whose deep center weighs no
    dark, but only heart,
Man in whom each man can find
    what's nearest to his heart,
the root of all his actions, mirroring
    life and death, gazing on human
    doings,

Man, ever to you I come, wading
    through the slender stream of
    history
going to meet each heart, each
    thought
(history is thronged with thoughts
    and death of hearts).
Your Body I seek for all of history,
Your depth it is I seek.[44]

Here, then, is the answer to the crucial question: the deepest meaning of history goes beyond history and finds its full explanation in Christ, the God-man. Christian hope projects itself beyond the limit of time. The Kingdom of God is grafted onto human history, and there it grows, but its goal is the life to come. Humanity is called to advance beyond death, even beyond time, toward the definitive onset of eternity alongside the glorious Christ in the communion of the Trinity. "Their hope is full of immortality" (Wis 3:4).

EPILOGUE

The final conversation took place in the small dining room of the Papal Palace at Castel Gandolfo. The Holy Father's secretary, Archbishop Stanisław Dziwisz, also took part.

26. "Someone Must Have Guided That Bullet"

What really happened on May 13, 1981? Did the assassination attempt and the events surrounding it reveal some truth about the Papacy, perhaps one previously overlooked? Is it possible to read in them a special message about your personal mission, Holy Father? You went to visit your assailant in prison, and you met him face to face. How do you view the events of those days now, after all these years? What significance have that attack and the events connected with it acquired in your life?

JOHN PAUL II: It was all a testimony to divine grace. I see here a certain similarity to the trials suffered by Cardinal Wyszyński during his imprisonment. The experience of the Primate of Poland, though, lasted more than three years, while my own lasted rather a short time, just a few months. Agca knew how to shoot, and he certainly shot to kill. Yet it was as if someone was guiding and deflecting that bullet.

STANISŁAW DZIWISZ: Agca shot to kill. That shot should have been fatal. The bullet passed through the Holy Father's body, wounding him in the stomach, the right elbow, and the left index finger. Then the bullet fell between the Pope and me. I heard two more shots, and two people standing near us were wounded.

I asked the Holy Father: "Where?" He replied: "In the stomach." "Does it hurt?" "It does."

There was no doctor within reach. There was no time to think. We immediately carried the Holy Father into an ambulance and set off at great speed toward the Gemelli Hospital. The Holy Father was praying *sotto voce*. Then, during the journey, he lost consciousness.

A number of factors would determine whether or not he survived, for example the question of time, the time it took us to reach the hospital: a few more minutes, some obstruction along the way, and it would have been too late. In all this, the hand of God is visible. Everything points toward it.

JOHN PAUL II: Yes, I remember that

journey to the hospital. For a short time I remained conscious. I had a sense that I would survive. I was in pain, and this was a reason to be afraid, but I had a strange trust. I said to Father Stanisław that I had forgiven my assailant. What happened at the hospital, I do not remember.

STANISŁAW DZIWISZ: Almost immediately after we arrived at the hospital, the Holy Father was taken into the operating room. The situation was very grave. The Holy Father had lost a great deal of blood. His blood pressure was falling dramatically, his pulse barely registered. The doctors suggested that I administer the Sacrament of the Sick. I did so at once.

JOHN PAUL II: I was already practically on the other side.

STANISŁAW DZIWISZ: Then he was given a blood transfusion.

JOHN PAUL II: The further complications and delays in the whole process of recovery can be traced back to that transfusion.

STANISŁAW DZIWISZ: The first blood was rejected, but there were doctors in the hospital who gave their own blood to the Holy Father. This second transfusion went well. The doctors who performed the operation did not expect the patient to survive. They paid no attention at all, understandably, to the finger which had been wounded by the bullet. "If he survives, we can do something about that later" they said to me. As it happened, the wounded finger healed by itself, without any treatment.

After the operation, the Holy Father was transferred to a recovery room. The doctors were afraid of infection, which in such a situation could have been lethal. Some of the Holy Father's internal organs were damaged. The operation had been very difficult. As it happened, everything healed perfectly, without the slightest complication, even though such complex operations frequently do lead to problems.

JOHN PAUL II: In Rome a dying Pope, in Poland mourning . . . In Kraków the university students organized a demonstration: the "white march."[45] When I went to Poland, I said: "I have come to thank you for the 'white march'." I also went to Fatima, to thank Our Lady.

O dear Lord! It was a hard experience. I didn't wake up until the following day, toward noon. And I said to Fr. Stanisław: "Yesterday I didn't say Compline."

STANISLAW DZIWISZ: To be precise, Holy Father, you asked me: "Have I said Compline?" You thought it was still the previous day.

JOHN PAUL II: I knew nothing of what Fr. Stanisław knew. They hadn't told me how serious the situation was. Besides, I was simply unconscious for quite some time. When I awoke, my morale was reasonably good. At least initially.

STANISLAW DZIWISZ: The next three days were awful. The Holy Father suffered greatly. He had tubes and cuts everywhere. Nevertheless, his recovery was quite fast. At the beginning of June, the Holy Father returned home. He wasn't even required to observe a special diet.

JOHN PAUL II: As you see, I have quite a strong constitution.

STANISLAW DZIWISZ: At a later stage, though, his system was attacked by a dangerous virus as a consequence of the first blood transfusion, or his general debilitated condition. The Holy Father had been given an enormous quantity of antibiotics to protect him against infection. This significantly weakened his natural immune system. That was how a further illness could develop. The Holy Father was returned to the hospital.

Thanks to intensive medical treatment, his state of health improved to the point where the doctors decided they could proceed to a further operation to complete the surgery carried out on the day of the attack. The Holy Father chose August 5 for this, the feast of Our Lady of the Snows, which is kept in the liturgical calendar as the Dedication of the Basilica of Saint Mary Major.

This second phase of treatment was equally successful. On August 13, three months after the attack, the doctors issued a medical bulletin to say that the hospital treatment had been concluded. The patient was definitively discharged from hospital.

Five months after the attack, the Holy Father returned to Saint Peter's Square to meet the faithful once again. He showed not a trace of fear, nor even of stress, although the doctors had warned that this was a possibility. He said on that occasion: "Again I have become indebted to the Blessed Virgin and to all the Patron Saints. Could I forget that the event in Saint Peter's Square took place on the day and at the hour when the first appearance of the Mother of Christ to the poor little peasants has been remembered for over sixty years at Fatima in Portugal? For, in everything that happened to me on that very day, I felt that extraordinary motherly protection and care, which turned out to be stronger than the deadly bullet."

JOHN PAUL II: Around Christmas 1983 I visited my attacker in prison. We spoke at length. Ali Agca, as everyone knows, was a professional assassin. This means that the attack was not his own initiative, it was someone else's idea; someone else had commissioned him to carry it out. In the course of our conversation it became clear that Ali Agca was still wondering how the attempted assassination could possibly have failed. He had planned it meticulously, attending to every tiny detail. And yet his intended victim had escaped death. How could this have happened?

The interesting thing was that his perplexity had led him to the religious question. He wanted to know about the secret of Fatima, and what the secret actually was. This was his principal concern; more than anything else, he wanted to know this.

Perhaps those insistent questions showed that he had grasped something really important. Ali Agca had probably sensed that over and above his own power, over and above the power of shooting and killing, there was a higher power. He then began to look for it. I hope and pray that he found it.

STANISŁAW DZIWISZ: I would describe the Holy Father's miraculous return to life and health as a gift from heaven. The attempted assassination, humanly speaking, has remained a mystery. Neither the trial nor the attacker's long imprisonment has clarified it. I witnessed the Holy Father's visit to Ali Agca in prison. The Pope had already forgiven him publicly in his first speech after the attack. On the prisoner's part I did not hear the words: "I ask for forgiveness." He was only interested in the secret of Fatima. The Holy Father received the attacker's mother and family on several occasions, and often inquired after him of the prison chaplains.

On the spiritual level, the mystery consists in the whole dramatic sequence of events, which weakened the health and strength of the Holy Father, but did not in any way impair the effectiveness and fruitfulness of his apostolic ministry in the

Church and in the world.

I do not consider it an exaggeration to apply in this case the famous saying: *Sanguis martyrum semen christianorum.*[46] Perhaps there was a need for that blood to be spilled in Saint Peter's Square, on the site of the martyrdom of the early Christians.

Without doubt, the first fruit of that blood was the union of the entire Church in prayer for the Pope's survival. Throughout the night following the attack, pilgrims who had come for the General Audience and an ever increasing number of local people prayed in Saint Peter's Square. In the following days, in cathedrals, in churches, and in chapels all over the world, Mass was celebrated and prayers were offered for the Pope's intentions. He himself said in this regard: "It is difficult for me to think of all this without emotion, without deep gratitude to everyone, to all those who gathered in prayer on the day of May 13, and to all those who persevered in it for all this time . . . I am grateful to Christ the Lord and to the Holy Spirit, who, through this event which took place in Saint Peter's Square on May 13 at 5:17 p.m., inspired so many hearts to common prayer. And thinking of this great prayer, I cannot forget the words of the Acts of the Apostles referring to Peter: 'Earnest prayer for him was made to God by the Church' (Acts 12:5)."[47]

JOHN PAUL II: I am constantly aware that in everything I say and do in fulfillment of my vocation, my mission, my ministry, what happens is not just my own initiative. I know that it is not I alone who act in what I do as the Successor of Peter.

Let us take the example of the Communist system. As I said earlier, a contributory factor in its demise was certainly its deficient economic doctrine, but to account for what happened solely in terms of economic factors would be a rather naive simplification. On the other hand, it would obviously be ridiculous to claim that the Pope brought down communism single-handedly.

I think the explanation can be found in the Gospel. When the first disciples returned to their Master, having been sent out on a mission, they said: "Lord, even the demons are subject to us in your name" (Lk 10:17). Christ replied to them: "Do not rejoice in this, that the spirits are subject to you, but rejoice that your names are written in heaven" (Lk 10:20). And on another occasion he adds: "Say: 'We are unworthy servants, we have only done what was our duty' " (Lk 17:10).

Unworthy servants . . . The sense of being an "unworthy servant" is growing in me in the midst of all that happens around me — and I think I feel at ease with this.

Let us return to the assassination attempt: I think it was one of the final convulsions of the arrogant ideologies unleashed during the twentieth century. Both fascism and nazism eliminated people. So did communism. Here in Italy, the practice of elimination continued, justifying itself by similar arguments: the Red Brigade killed innocent and honest men.

In rereading the transcriptions of those conversations of some years ago, I would note that the manifestations of violence from the so-called *anni di piombo* (years of lead) have been significantly reduced. Yet in recent years the world has seen the rise of so-called "terror networks" that place the lives of millions of innocent people under constant threat. Striking confirmation of this was provided by the destruction of the Twin Towers in New York (September 11, 2001), the bomb blast in Atocha Station in Madrid (March 11, 2004), and the slaughter at Beslan in North Ossetia (September 1–3, 2004). Where are these new eruptions of violence leading?

The demise first of nazism and then of the Soviet Union signaled a failure. It revealed the utter absurdity of the large-scale violence that formed part of the theory and practice of those systems. Will we be able to learn from the dramatic lessons of history? Or will we be prey once more to the passions at work in the human spirit, yielding yet again to the evil promptings of violence?

Believers know that the presence of evil is always accompanied by the presence of good, by grace. As Saint Paul wrote: "The free gift is not like the trespass. For if the many died through the one man's trespass, much more surely have the grace of God and the free gift in the grace of the one man, Jesus Christ, abounded for the many" (Rom 5:15). These words retain their relevance today. Redemption is ongoing. Where evil grows, there the hope for good also grows. In our times evil has grown disproportionately, operating through perverted systems which have practiced violence and elimination on a vast scale. I am not speaking here of evil committed by individuals for personal motives or through individual initiatives. The evil of the twentieth century was not a small-scale evil, it was not simply "homemade." It was an evil of gigantic proportions, an evil which availed itself of state structures in order to accomplish its wicked work, an evil built up into a system.

At the same time, however, divine grace has been superabundantly revealed. There is no evil from which God cannot draw forth a greater good. There is no suffering which he cannot transform into a path leading to him. Offering himself freely in his passion and death on the Cross, the Son of God took upon himself all the evil of sin. The suffering of the Crucified God is not just one form of suffering alongside others, not just another more or less painful ordeal: it is an unequaled suffering. In sacrificing himself for us all, Christ gave a new meaning to suffering, opening up a new dimension, a new order: the order of love. It is true that suffering entered human history with original sin. Sin is that "sting" (cf. 1 Cor 15:55–56) which inflicts pain, wounding man mortally. Yet the passion of Christ on the Cross gave a radically new meaning to suffering, transforming it from within. It introduced into human history, which is the history of sin, a blameless suffering accepted purely for love. This suffering opens the door to the hope of liberation, hope for the definitive elimination of that "sting," which is tearing humanity apart. It is this suffering which burns and consumes evil with the flame of love and draws forth even from sin a great flowering of good.

All human suffering, all pain, all infirmity contains within itself a promise of salvation, a promise of joy: "I am now rejoicing in my sufferings for your sake," writes Saint Paul (Col 1:24). This applies to all forms of suffering, called forth by evil. It applies to that enormous social and political evil which divides and torments the world today: the evil of war, the evil of oppression afflicting individuals and peoples, the evil of social injustice, of human dignity trodden underfoot, of racial and religious discrimination, the evil of violence, terrorism, the arms race — all this evil is present in the world partly so as to awaken our love, our self-gift in generous and disinterested service to those visited by suffering. In the love that pours forth from the heart of Christ, we find hope for the future of the world. Christ has redeemed the world: "By his wounds we are healed" (Is 53:5).

Notes

1. *De civitate Dei* XIV, 28.
2. Cf. *Między heroizmem a bestialstwem* (*Between Heroism and Bestiality*), Częstochowa, 1984.
3. "A part of that force which always desires evil and always accomplishes good" (*Faust*, Part I, Scene 3: "In the Study").
4. No. 13.
5. Pastoral constitution *Gaudium et Spes*, 37.
6. Ibid., 2.
7. *Adversus haereses*, IV, 20, 7.
8. Cf. nos. 6–27.
9. No. 36.
10. *Grundlegung zur Metaphysik der Sitten*, in *Werke*, iv (Darmstadt, 1956), 51.
11. Ibid., 61.
12. © The Grail (England). Used with permission.
13. *Promethidion. Rzecz w dwóch dialogach z epilogiem*, in Cyprian Norwid, *Pisma wszystkie*, iii: *Poematy* (Warsaw, 1971), 440.
14. The Piast dynasty ruled from 960 to

1379. It was the first Polish dynasty, but it only began to be designated with this name from the seventeenth century onward. [Ed.]

15. Kievan Rus was initially (at the end of the ninth century) a collection of Slav principalities grouped around the leading figure of the prince of Kiev. Gradually Rus expanded to cover a territory reaching from Kiev in the south to Novgorod in the north. From the early years of the tenth century there is documentary evidence of commercial contacts with the Byzantine world. Later, cultural contacts also developed, through which Christianity first came to be proclaimed in the land of Kiev. The baptism of Prince Vladimir led to the systematic spread of Christianity throughout the principality, which then became the center from which the Gospel was carried to much of the Slav world. [Ed.]

16. Stanisław Wyspiański, *Wyzwolenie*, in *Dzieła zebrane*, v (Kraków, 1959), 98.

17. *Lumen Gentium*, 13.

18. Cf. Karol Wojtyła, *Poezje (Poems)*, (Kraków, 1998), 212. The verses quoted have been translated specially for this publication.

19. Cf. ibid., 214–220.

20. Founded in 1190 by German merchants and pilgrims during the siege of Acre

in the Third Crusade, it was originally called the Order of the Brothers of the Hospital of Our Lady of the Teutons. In 1198 it became a military order whose members, all from the nobility, took vows of poverty, chastity, and obedience. In the thirteenth century, the order moved toward eastern Europe, gaining distinction in the fight against the Mongols in Hungary (1211–1225) and against the pagan Slavs of northeastern Europe. Later it formed a full-fledged monastic-military state, Prussia, its territory bounded by the Baltic Sea, the Oder, and the Neva. The expansion of the Teutonic Knights toward the east was halted when they were defeated by Alexander Nevsky's army in 1240. A decisive moment for the Order was its defeat in 1410 by the Polish and Lithuanian armies at the battle of Grunwald, which marked the beginning of its decline. [Ed.]

21. Nos. 6, 7, 14: *L'Osservatore Romano*, English edition (June 23, 1980), 9–12.

22. The Jagiellonian dynasty ruled not only in Poland (1386–1572), but also for certain periods in Lithuania, Hungary, and Bohemia. The name comes from Władysław Jagiełło (1350–1434), grand duke of Lithuania, who married Hedwig, queen of Poland, thereby favoring the con-

version of Lithuania to Christianity and contributing to that country's union with Poland.

23. Cf. *Pensées*, ed. Brunschvicg, 347.

24. On May 3, 1791 the "Diet of Four Years" promulgated a constitutional charter that was, in effect, the first written constitution in Europe. [Ed.]

25. *Gaudium et Spes*, 22.

26. Ibid.

27. Ibid.

28. Ibid.

29. Ibid.

30. No. 14.

31. No. 22.

32. Ibid.

33. Cf. *Lumen Gentium*, 8; *Gaudium et Spes*, 43; *Unitatis redintegratio*, 6.

34. Cf. Pastoral constitution *Gaudium et Spes*, 2.

35. No. 76.

36. *Summa Theologiae*, I–II, q. 90, a. 4.

37. There was a heavy price to pay for victory: the city of Legnica was completely destroyed by the Mongols, who then decided to withdraw. [Ed.]

38. This is a reference to the pamphlet *Satira* by Johannes Falkenburg, in which the Teutonic Order was defended in somewhat polemical terms against the king of

Poland. The text was suspected to be heretical and condemned by the Council. [Ed.]

39. Jasna Góra (in Latin *Clarus Mons*) is considered the "national shrine" because of the light that the Poles have always drawn from the icon of the Black Madonna venerated there in the dark times of wars and foreign occupations. Ever since the fifteenth century, Jasna Góra has been the most visited shrine in Poland. At the time of the Swedish invasion (1655), which is known in Polish history as the "flood," the cloister of the shrine became a fortress that the invader did not succeed in conquering. The nation read this event as a promise of victory in the recurring dark experiences of history (cf. John Paul II, *Rise, Let Us Be On Our Way*, New York 2004, 51–53). [Ed.]

40. This consisted in the right of every member of the parliament (*sejm*) to oppose a law or even the work of an entire legislative session, rendering it null and void. According to traditional law, the Polish nobility were politically equal among themselves, and every parliamentary law had to be unanimously approved. The *liberum veto,* used for the first time in 1652, was practiced with increasing frequency in subsequent years, until it paralyzed the Polish political system. After repeated at-

tempts, it was finally eliminated by the constitution of May 3, 1791. [Ed.]

41. Cf. note 24, page 171.

42. *Lumen Gentium*, 63.

43. No. 22.

44. Karol Wojtyła, *Easter Vigil, 1966*, in *Poezje* (*Poems*), 180. The verses quoted have been translated specially for this publication.

45. This is a reference to the procession held at Kraków on the Sunday following the attempted assassination. Tens of thousands of students and citizens took part, all dressed in white, to symbolize their opposition to the darkness of evil and violence. From Błonia Square, the procession made its way in silence along Trzech Wieszczów Street, Karmelicka Street and Szewska Street, as far as Market Square (Rynek), where at noon, Cardinal Franciszek Macharski, Archbishop of Kraków, celebrated Mass.

46. "The blood of martyrs is the seed of Christians."

47. Catechesis at the General Audience of October 7, 1981, par. 5: *L'Osservatore Romano*, English edition (October 12, 1981), 3.